Managing the Difficult. Zero Tolerance

Proven Strategies for Managing Difficult People

The contents of this book may not be reproduced, duplicated or transmitted without direct written permission from the author.

Under no circumstances will any legal responsibility or blame be held against the publisher for any reparation, damages, or monetary loss due to the information herein, either directly or indirectly.

Legal Notice:

This book is copyright protected. This is only for personal use. You cannot amend, distribute, sell, use, quote or paraphrase any part or the content within this book without the consent of the author.

Disclaimer Notice:

Please note the information contained within this document is for educational and entertainment purposes only. Every attempt has been made to provide accurate, up to date and reliable complete information. No warranties of any kind are expressed or implied. Readers acknowledge that the author is not engaging in the rendering of legal, financial, medical or professional advice. The content of this book has been derived from various sources. Please consult a licensed professional before attempting any techniques outlined in this book.

By reading this document, the reader agrees that under no circumstances are is the author responsible for any losses, direct or indirect, which are incurred as a result of the use of information contained within this document, including, but not limited to, —errors, omissions, or inaccuracies.

© Copyright 2019. All rights reserved.

Contents

PREFACE 1
   How to Use This Book 4
   About the Author 4

CHAPTER 1: PROBLEMATIC PEOPLE—COMMON NEGATIVE BEHAVIOURS 7
   Types of Difficult People 9
   Thinking Time 22
   Summary 22

CHAPTER 2: GET YOUR HEAD OUT OF THE SAND— TACKLING THE PROBLEM 25
   Thinking Time 32
   Summary 33

CHAPTER 3: CONTROL YOURSELF—MANAGING YOUR EMOTIONS 35
   Managing Your Bias 36
   Controlling Your Emotions 41
   Management Styles: X vs. Y 45
   Thinking Time 47
   Summary 48

CHAPTER 4: THE BIG TALK—CONFRONTING THE ISSUE .. 51
   The Zero Tolerance Steps 52
   What Not to Do? 58
   SBR vs. BFE 59
   Thinking Time 61

SUMMARY 62

CHAPTER 5: THE ROAD AHEAD—MAKING PROGRESS ...65
OBSERVE AND NOTE PROGRESS 66
BEHAVIOURS TO AVOID...68
LEARN HOW TO GIVE NEGATIVE FEEDBACK...........................72
THINKING TIME 77

CHAPTER 6: WHAT DO YOU SAY—ULTIMATUMS AND CHECK-UPS 79
THINKING TIME 84
SUMMARY 85

CHAPTER 7: FAILURE AND FALLOUT—WHEN TO TERMINATE 87
THE SOCIOLOGY OF GROUPS 88
WHEN TO TERMINATE 93
THINKING TIME 104
SUMMARY 104

CHAPTER 8: WHEN THEY'RE NOT YOUR EMPLOYEE— CLIENTS, PARTNERS, AND BOSSES 107
WHEN YOUR CLIENT IS BEING DIFFICULT 108
WHEN YOUR PARTNER IS BEING DIFFICULT.........................117
WHEN YOUR BOSS IS BEING DIFFICULT 122
THINKING TIME 128
SUMMARY 128

CONCLUSION 131

REFERENCES 135

Preface

We've all had our fair share of difficult people to deal with—they are out there, and they can definitely ruin your day, your week, your month.

Most of the times, difficult people don't necessarily realise just how much of a strain they put on their relationships with everyone else—they just *do* the things they do, without caring too much about the toxicity of their behaviour.

On the other side of the fence, those who have to deal with toxic people risk too much when they don't do anything about it. Allowing yourself to be swamped in negativity is just a surefire way to failure—failure to run your daily tasks properly, failure to achieve your goals, and, eventually, failure to live up to your other employees' expectations. For some or with time, that might also be failure to not be a toxic boss yourself.

When it comes to dealing with this kind of people, the Zero Tolerance approach is the single best use of your energy—especially when it comes to the workplace. You just risk too much leaving toxic behaviours unaddressed.

However, **it is of the utmost importance to understand that the Zero Tolerance approach is not**

about treating your employees poorly. It's the contrary, actually. There is nothing more self-destructive and more short-lived than not cooperating well with the people who work with and for you. Taking this route will only make things worse from every point of view, as it will make you seem too strict, too authoritarian and, well, too much of a micro-manager. Doing this will only make your employees replicate your behaviour and thus will create further negative interactions. Before you know it, everything can spiral out of control and ruin everything for you and for your employees, too.

The *good* Zero Tolerance approach, however, is all about confronting the issues, rather than burying your head in the sand. No matter what problems may come your way and no matter how small or not so small they may be, they cannot simply be ignored. Leaving them "be" will only lead to negative behaviours getting entrenched in the culture of your company. Soon enough, the unity and functionality of your team will be in jeopardy.

Zero Tolerance is about tackling issues when they arise, based on the full knowledge and support you need. This is precisely why it is crucial to learn how to identify, address, and correct problematic employee behaviours.

This is what this book aims to do—teach you about the healthy Zero Tolerance approach and everything it entails. As you will see, each chapter in this book is dedicated to explaining every step of the way in the Zero

Tolerance strategy. Every chapter will end with questions or mini-exercises meant to help you think of your own experience, as well as how you can apply the information offered in that given chapter to your own particular situation.

Fail to prepare, prepare to fail. Even if you are not facing negative behaviours in your team right now, it is still important that you know how to tackle issues as they arise, in the most tactful and efficient ways.

And when it comes to that, the book at hand will definitely help!

Who is this book for? In short, this book is for everyone who has ever had to deal with negative behaviours in the workplace—and anyone who thinks they might spot sprouts of this kind of behaviour as well.

If you are any kind of boss or manager, you will love this book and the step-by-step guide provided in it.

If you are a team leader or supervisor, you will definitely appreciate all the advice meant to help you create a better, healthier, more efficient team by eliminating the negativity prowling the workspace.

If you are an aspiring manager or if you study management, this book will help you understand what management is truly about (and maybe more importantly, what it isn't about, too).

If you are an entrepreneur or an entrepreneur to be, you will find this book to be useful in the realisation of your goals, as it will help you build a better, healthier, more productive team where negative behaviours will never feel at home.

How to Use This Book

The book at hand is designed to function the way a manual relays, step by step, the actions you should take to make sure you achieve success in your Zero Tolerance approach. While we definitely encourage you to read it from the first page to the last, do know that flipping through the different sections is doable, and it can help you understand some basic concepts about the Zero Tolerance approach.

About the Author

When I started writing this book, I knew what I needed to say. And while I was typing out my ideas, I realised that, well, people might not want to listen to me—why would you, after all? Who is this buffoon telling you what to do and what not to do when it comes to *your* team?

To understand why you should trust my expertise, you

should first understand that I have years and years of actual, hands-on experience in managing businesses. But maybe even more than that, I have experience in managing people.

I know how teams function and what drives them forward.

By profession, I am a Construction Manager. I have delivered projects worth millions of British pounds without having actual, formal training in management. I manage more than a hundred tradesmen, contractors, workmen and women from all walks of life, on a daily basis. From the educated Engineers, Health and Safety officers, and Directors to the ex-con Scaffolder covered in tattoos and attitude problems, I have managed them all.

And to be frank, I have loved every single second of it.

It isn't always easy, but the rewards far exceed any kind of whining I could do about how difficult it is to manage so many people who are very frequently so different—when compared to me and when compared to the rest of the team, as well.

You should take my advice because I have actual, practical experience when it comes to everything I say here. I have tried and tested all the tactics and techniques presented in this book in my own skin—so I know exactly what works and what doesn't. I have managed to manage (!) extremely difficult people precisely because of my trial and error cycle.

The great news is that you don't have to try and fail and then try again—not when you are holding this book in your hands, that is. I have created a series of steps based on adaptive techniques that can function in multiple situations, with multiple types of difficult people, and with multiple types of managers as well. If you put these things into action in the ways that I describe, you should enjoy a high level of success.

I truly hope you will make good use of all the tips I present here. These are genuinely good pieces of advice—things I have learned from my own experience, and things that I genuinely hope will help others as well.

As an author, and as a Manager, I wish this book to be *useful* to you in every sense there is!

Chapter 1

Problematic People—Common Negative Behaviours

Just like weeds in a flower garden, problematic people come in many shapes. Some are tacitly negative, spitting venom over water cooler conversations, others are obnoxious and loud, interrupting you in the middle of meetings with issues that are far less grand in importance as what you are trying to convey.

The bad news is that you have to learn how to determine what kind of negative behaviour every person in your team is prone to. This can be a journey of self-discovery, but maybe more than that, it can be a journey of learning about what humans are at their worst: envious, mean, angry, frustrated, and way too willing to ditch their neighbours (i.e. their teammates) into the abyss.

The good news is that humans are not inherently bad—I refuse to think so, and it is really important for you to start with this mindset because it will help you genuinely believe in the power of the techniques you employ.

What that good news actually means is that you can *change* negative behaviours, as they most often sprout from an underlying issue—one which you can help solve.

Truth be told, you will always encounter people you are simply not compatible with, and that is perfectly OK. We are meant to be different, and it's one of the things that makes life so exciting. Regardless of whether these people have an attitude problem, they don't match their goals with yours, or there is simply something about you that rubs them the wrong way, you will always have to deal with these kinds of individuals. In your personal life, you can frequently turn around and move to greener pastures.

But when you are a manager handling these people, it is your responsibility to not only deal with them, but also try to correct their lacking behaviours.

It is of the utmost importance that you do this as soon as possible. Unfortunately, negativity spreads like the plague, so it is essential that you take action sooner, rather than later. Not addressing these issues (and not addressing them in time) can only lead to further problems.

The Zero Tolerance approach is here to help you with this—and to add to the good news, it is really not that difficult to learn the basics behind this theory.

It all starts with identifying the types of difficult people you have to deal with. So, without further ado, let's dive in and learn more about this.

Types of Difficult People

Everyone is different, and that is one of the truly wonderful things about life and the people you meet along the way.

However, in this diverse garden of people with whom you will have to interact in your life, you will also find several overarching "profiles"—archetypes that share common themes. Here are some of the most common ones:

The Chronic Complainer

This is your average Sally who doesn't like *anything*. From the moment she arrives at work to the moment she leaves it, it seems that all she does is complain, complain, complain—and then complain some more.

To this person, there's nothing good about the place she works in, about the people she works with, about the tasks she runs on a daily basis. It seems that there's nothing that could make her even slightly happier. But no matter how miserable her complaints reveal her to be, she will *not* resign the job under any circumstances.

Unnecessarily negative about everything under the sun, the average Sally (who might as well be the average Saul) will complain about everything: from her paycheck to the size of her desk, the buttons on the microwave, and even the quality of the toilet paper at the office.

Looking at this person as an outsider might seem funny at times—her complaining is so chronic that she seems like a comedy character, rather than a real person.

The problem here lies in the fact that she *is* a real person, working with other real people, for a real business. And her constant complaining makes everyone else uncomfortable at the very least and complicit at the very worst.

This person damages the team's cohesion and morale, spreading her pessimism around, constantly nitpicking everything, and being quick to bring up every minor issue, shortcoming or failing.

Of course, some negative people don't even realise just how harmful their behaviour is. The Chronic Complainer falls into this category. They complain out of habit more than anything, but they don't fully realise the extent to which their negativity influences the workplace.

Solution: Most of the times, the Chronic Complainer does not necessarily *want* to be this way. Therefore, having a clear and heartfelt discussion with him/her might actually touch their soft side. Try to steer them towards positivity, rather than negativity. Praise their achievements and the achievements of the teams they are in every time they happen. Try to address complaints that are reasonable (and don't cost your business too much). Show them you can take a positive attitude, so that they can do it too. In general, however, it might be best if you don't assign leadership positions to this person—their chronic complaining might get worse, and it might affect team members too much.

The Tardy Sloth

This person is always late.

Late with everything.

They are late to work, they are late at meetings, they are late delivering tasks, and they are late at everything they do.

In many ways, this person is like a lazy, unorganised, forgetful sloth—one you cannot rely on and one you cannot properly manage, whatever you try.

At their very worst, the Tardy Sloth might not even show up at all.

Clearly, this kind of behaviour is unfair towards everyone else who puts their efforts into doing everything right (and on time!). And even more clearly, this type of attitude needs to be addressed, preferably with as little tardiness as possible.

Solution: This person's issue is frequently a problem related to habit and how they are used to doing things. Sometimes, they might be insubordinate and rebel, but most times, they are late by habit. Have a good discussion with them, explaining to them the repercussions of their actions and just how much they (and the entire team) is losing as a result of their tardiness. If needed, give them an ultimate deadline to change their behaviour and tell them you will have to cut their paycheck or even let them go if the problem persists.

The Antisocial Moth

This person could have been a social butterfly—but they don't like people all that much. And that's OK, too. In the end, we are not all obliged to be ultra-social and friendly with everyone.

The main issue with this person is that, at their extreme version, they tend to formulate any kind of request as if it's a military drill. In addition, they tend to show other types of antisocial behaviours too, and this only puts a strain on your team, who might find communicating with this person difficult. As a consequence, tasks will be delivered poorly, and team morale will drop.

Needless to say, you need to address this type of behaviour as much as you need to address any other type of negative behaviour. It's one thing to not be the social butterfly of the workspace, but when your lack of communication skills affects everyone around you, an intervention is needed. And the best person that intervention should come from is none other than the manager of the team.

Solution: Communicating with this person is very difficult, so it's important to be as tactful as you can. They might be extreme introverts, or they might simply not like their jobs. Try to talk to these people and see why they don't communicate properly. Bring it to their attention that their attitude is hurting other people and the entire process. Talk to them and ask them if they have any kind of problem at home that might make them difficult at work. And if everything else fails, issue a warning. There's just no way you can deal with this any other way.

The Workplace Thief

The Thief is not necessarily a thief per se, although don't be surprised if office supplies keep on disappearing on his watch.

Rather than that, the Thief is someone who constantly makes costly mistakes in their work. One mistake will usually not cost the business too much, but a second, third, and one hundredth mistake *will* cost you quite a lot of money every year. You could use that money in so many amazing ways, but instead this person is (probably more or less consciously) stealing from your business.

More often than not, this person is also a Manipulator (another type of negative person in the workplace), and their issue is usually connected to an underlying problem, like lack of respect, bad attitude, or poor work ethic.

Solution: Chances are that this person knows what they are doing, particularly if they show Manipulator traits as well. Therefore, your Zero Tolerance approach when it comes to them should be, well, quite extreme. Talk to them about their problem, create a plan with them to follow over the course of three months and analyse the results afterwards. If they don't show improvement, expect to have to let them go, based on lack of adherence to company Code of Conduct.

The Roaring Rebel

This is not a rebel in the sense that he challenges the status-quo, or that he goes against the mainstream with unique, cutting-edge ideas.

No, this person is bad to the bone. They spread venom and they have a major attitude problem when it comes to pretty much everything work-related. They rarely respect authority and they are incredibly difficult and intimidating to handle—precisely because every attempt at discussing the matter with them quickly escalates into something that resembles the provocations between rival fans at a soccer game.

Many times, this person will also have problems with tardiness and workplace theft, which make matters even worse—and it makes it even more urgent that you handle the situation.

Solution: It is incredibly difficult to deal with this type of person because they will meet every communication effort with their hands folded over their chest, aggressiveness, and disregard. The best way to handle the situation is to give them an ultimatum and let them go if they don't address their behaviour. You simply cannot (and shouldn't be obliged to) keep this kind of people around.

The Vicious Victim and Mean Manipulator

This is one of the worst types of bad behaviour in the workplace because it unleashes its negativity in more than one way: their entire attitude towards work and everyone is simply vicious.

Most of the times, these people do what they do with full awareness, which makes it even worse. Also most of the time, these people are a bit more difficult to "locate," because their destructive ways are usually very well covered.

This person is always a victim. They didn't do anything wrong, Mark in Accounting did. They didn't say anything wrong to the client, they were just relaying what Lucy told them. They are the victim in all situations. But, in fact, they scheme and they sow discord between team members like it's their favorite game. On top of everything, this person gossips a lot—and on most occasions, their gossiping ruins reputations, it ruins other people's trustworthiness, and it damages the cohesiveness of the entire team.

This person is like a snake, hissing out venom everywhere they turn. They need to be handled very tactfully, otherwise they might turn on you and spread gossip about you amongst all of the other employees.

Solution: As with the Workplace Thief, this person should be handled with an ultimatum. However, you need to put a lot of attention into the words you use because you don't want to turn them against you and give them another three months to spread their venom around (this time, even more aggressively). Try to find if there is something really bothering them. Like most bullies, these people might have underlying issues, and while you might not be a psychologist competent to work through every cause of frustration, the best you can do is have an honest chat with the person before you give them the ultimatum.

The Constant Patient

This person might actually have health issues, but in the last two months, they showed up to work for a total of four weeks and two days. The remaining days, they were off— every time due to a different ailment.

Dealing with this kind of person is very difficult because, well, they might *actually* be sick, and you want to be understanding with them.

However, when their productivity is heavily affected by the constant sickness, it is time to address this problem. The first step is to ask them for medical proof every time they request time off.

The second one is to check with your state's legislation regarding how many days a person can be sick every year for you to be allowed to replace them.

It sounds harsh, but unless there is real, palpable medical proof, it's also hard to believe that someone suffers from colds twice a month, stomach problems every three weeks, and heavy headaches every other day. Yes, this might be possible, and I'm not saying that you should fire someone who is actually sick.

But the (also) harsh truth is that most of the times, the Constant Patient is a Constant Netflix Binger, so you should address them as soon as possible.

Solution: You need to be very delicate here, because if the person is actually sick, you will come out badly. If the person isn't and you allow them to manipulate you further on, you will come out badly too. The best way to handle the problem is to ask for medical certifications every time they need time off for medical reasons (and this should be a blanket policy for your team). If they fail to provide the medical evidence, you can give them a serious warning, emphasising the fact that you understand that sickness happens, but that you need to know if you can rely on them further on.

The Ghostly Slacker

This person might look like they work. They sometimes send an email or two, they show up to meetings, and most of the time, they even show up to work on time.

Yet when you look at how they are aiming for their KPIs, you realise that there is something wrong about the way they manage their time.

It almost feels like this person is a ghostly apparition, despite them being at work every day, almost mimicking the fact that they work.

Obviously, this person isn't being fair towards all the other co-workers who are there every day in every sense of the word. So their negative behaviour might soon enough become contagious. If their deskmate sees them constantly scrolling through Facebook and endlessly watching YouTube videos of cats and sees that nothing is done to fix this, they might soon become a Slacker themselves. Eventually, this can turn into a snowball effect that will damage the productivity of the entire team.

Solution: You simply cannot allow someone to watch videos all day and still get their paycheck the same way their hard-working teammates do. Have a serious talk with this person and show them actual performance-related numbers. Ask for explanations: Why is it that they always seem like working, but fail to deliver the expected results? Why is it that they can't reach their KPIs? They might have actual problems at home, and you should definitely show support and understanding, emphasizing the fact that you cannot allow them to be slacking off for much longer. Unfortunately, the Zero Tolerance approach applies the same for everyone, so it is very important to accentuate the fact that it is not fair towards the other employees that this person continues with their lacking behaviour.

The Smartie Pants

This person might be smart indeed, but most of the time, the way they relay their knowledge to you and to other members of the team feels like an offence.

And the sad truth is that it most likely is intended to feel this way, because this negative person believes themselves to be above everyone. They are spotless, they know better, they know everything about everything, and they will not miss any opportunity to brag about it in any way.

The issue with this person is that he/she makes everyone else feel frustrated to the point where they will just give up. You should address this type of behaviour, even if the person at fault is actually productive, smart, and proactive. Yes, they might be great workers and they might perform excellently, but if their behaviour is affecting everyone else's efficiency and positivity, it just won't matter anymore.

Solution: This person might take it really badly if you bluntly tell them they are too arrogant and aggressive, so be sure to be delicate in your discussion with them. Tell them that other people are bothered by mean remarks and by the fact that this person seems to be the only one standing in the spotlight. At the same time, make sure to distribute your attention towards everyone else in the team. Since the Smartie Pants is a person feeding off praises, sharing your praises equally with the other team members will eventually tone her down in a natural way. And, well, if nothing changes, be prepared to actually let this person go—their negativity might affect the entire team way too much for the whole situation to be worth it.

The Egomaniac

This person cannot work in a team.

They just cannot cooperate. Sometimes, they are also antisocial, but even when they aren't, their egocentric nature prevents them from properly communicating with everyone else on the team. Most of the times, this person is also a Smartie Pants, at least to some extent.

Unless their work can be redistributed to tasks that are more individual in nature, it is really important to address the lacks of cooperation, communication, and team spirit this person shows. It is quite obvious why this person will affect everyone else around them and why some other people might just get sick of it.

Solution: This person is very similar to the Smartie Pants, and the two typologies frequently overlap. So, to make sure their negativity doesn't affect everyone else, handle them in a way similar to the Smartie Pants. Talk to them and make a concentrated effort to spread your praises and attention towards the other members of the crew.

Thinking Time

Chances are that you have interacted with at least one of the negative behaviours described in this chapter. What type of difficult person profile was it? How did you deal with them?

Is there anyone on your team right now who might fit these traits, and, if so, are they a clear typology, or a combination of multiple typologies?

Summary

Like it or not (probably *not*), difficult people are out there. Some of them are intentionally negative, others are just the result of a series of frustrations and problems (at a career and at a personal level too).

Spotting the typology is very important because it will help you manage them properly, even when management feels beyond hope (like in the case of the Rebel, for example). The Zero Tolerance approach is all about not tolerating bad behaviours, but addressing them as soon as possible.

My recommendation is to give people a chance to make things better, but it is also very important to be crystal clear about the repercussions of not fixing one's behaviour. Yes, that might mean that you have to let some people go, and it might mean you have to cut other people's paychecks in as much as half of it.

But Zero Tolerance needs to be *zero tolerance* across the entire team. Even when someone is really cute and even when you know for a fact they can do better, there's zero benefit to further tolerating the kind of behaviour that affects not only *one* person's productivity and efficiency, but the entire team's.

Handle everything with a dose of positivity. Most people can turn around and be better. They can stop being late to work. They can stop gossiping. They can stop slacking.

But they need to be motivated in that direction - and that is *your* job as a manager.

Chapter 2

Get Your Head Out of the Sand—Tackling the Problem

The worst part about dealing with negative people in the workplace is that they can turn you and the other persons in the same workplace into negative thinkers and doers.

Even the mere fact that you don't take action against an issue can be, well, an issue in itself, and a type of negative behaviour like slacking and not caring too much (which will in turn lead to a domino effect where everyone else will catch on to various types of negative behaviour).

Before you know it, your entire work life could turn into a living, personal Hell: one where you have to wake up every morning to go to your job, be surrounded by people who manipulate, complain, and simply don't do their work, and turn yourself into the Ogre of the entire workplace by taking an approach that is too authoritarian.

Sometimes, heads might roll in the process of cleaning out the weeds in a workplace—but that doesn't mean you have to turn into the Tyrant of your business. Eventually, that will simply make people leave—and you can't have a productive team without, well, *an actual team.*

Yes, people come and people go, but when this turns into a chronic disease of your business, you will soon find yourself out of resources, spending most of your time trying to build teams that shatter into pieces as soon as a bigger challenge comes along.

Living under a rock as a manager is not a solution; it is, unfortunately, one of the root causes of any company whose employees are simply underperforming.

It is of the utmost importance that you take your head out of the sand and start looking at the danger lying ahead of you. As a manager, you simply have no other option. You absolutely *have to* do it, no matter how uncomfortable or downright scared it might make you feel. You have to do it for your business, for all the hard work you have put into building a team, for the team itself!

The chapter at hand is meant to help you take the first steps towards success in handling difficult employees. Look at this as a sort of *prepping* for what is to come, because (I won't lie) it *will* be difficult.

Let's analyse the first things you should do to make sure

you are successful in this direction. Ask four questions and then put some things on paper.

1. Do you have a problem?

Sometimes, you might randomly spot negative behaviours in your workplace and, if you have had a bad experience with these kinds of issues before, you might feel a little paranoid about wanting to address every small mishap right away.

To make sure you don't start tossing ultimatums around like they're candy before you actually have a case, it is important to stop for a moment and think: Is the incident you are looking at isolated, or is it a repeated behaviour influencing your entire business? Could it be that it was an accident, a mistake, or simply part of a bigger problem connected to the business and not necessarily to the person in question?

For instance, if one of your employees is late a couple of times, this might not be a chronic issue. It might be that they simply had problems; it might be an accident. If, however, the same employees is late four or five times in a row, it is perhaps better if you start thinking of a solution for this problem. It doesn't have to be something very strict from the very beginning; start with a friendly warning and see where it goes.

2. What sort of Difficult Personality Profile do you have to deal with?

Many times, it is actually quite difficult to categorise a person as one archetype or another. Yet knowing this is important, so that you know how to tackle the problem the right way.

Take your time and gather information, observing your difficult employee in a variety of situations and interactions. Taking the time to study your employee will give you insight to determine exactly who you have to deal with. It is a crucial step towards success, really. And keep in mind that you don't only have to do this with your problem employees. Wouldn't it make you a better manager of everyone on your team if you took some time to watch and take note of what you see? You'll also relieve a lot of stress when you do have a problem if you've already done a lot of this legwork throughout the entire time your difficult person has worked with you.

3. Is there any chance they have an underlying reason for their behaviour?

Sometimes, people have problems outside of the workplace which they inadvertently bring into it. For instance, if someone used to be on time every day at work and has suddenly started to be late on a recurrent basis, it might be that they are going through something.

Likewise, if someone shows extreme antisocial behaviours, it might be that they have a psychological issue they are trying to deal with.

The point here is that you should give everyone the benefit of the doubt. No matter how great they might be, people are prone to being, well, *human*, so they might be going through things that affect them and their performance regardless of how much they try to control it.

Talk to people. Listen. Try to understand if there is an underlying issue and, if possible, help. Everyone should help other people in need!

This is also one reason why many employers provide free and confidential counselling or mental health services to employees as part of their benefits packages. If your company offers such a benefit, make sure your employees know about it, encourage them to use it if they have a need, and work to reduce the stigma that surrounds receiving such services.

4. Do you fully understand the repercussions of their behaviour?

Sometimes, you might feel tempted to dismiss bad behaviours, as there are other, more pressing matters to handle. What you need to understand, however, is that allowing negativity to roam free in your workplace is a really bad idea from every point of view. People will stop seeing pleasure in what they do, they will start slacking off at the best, and they will eventually turn negative themselves.

In the same way that you observed the behaviours of your difficult employee to determine his/her Difficult Personality Profile, so also can you observe the way other people respond or react. It shouldn't take long for you to recognize the impact a difficult person is having on your team.

Don't allow yourself to accept defeat and say "Ah, that's just how Sally is, she will complain about anything" and then go about your normal business matters. Address the situation before it becomes a full-fledged epidemic!

5. Create paper trails.

The only way to maintain your sanity and stop thinking that you might be crazy to spot bad behaviours everywhere is by creating actual paper trails to document what is happening: reports and notes about incidents.

It might sound like you're the crazy boss keeping a spreadsheet with everyone's mistakes, but it is actually necessary for you to do this so that you can make your case when the time comes. Yes, it might not be the most pleasant thing to do, but there's simply no other way.

Don't make this harder for yourself than is absolutely necessary. Create an easy tracking system that will allow you to pull up the proof when needed. One of the easiest ways to do this is by creating a spreadsheet with the following columns:

- Name

- Type of issue/ type of negative behaviour

- Incident 1 (date it and add a quick description, as well as references to whatever documentation you might need to support your argument, such as logging times for someone who is late or KPIs for someone who is slacking, as well as whether or not there are witnesses to support the argument)

- Incident 2 (same type of information as above)

- Incident 3 (same type of information as above)

- Incident 4 (same type of information as above)

- Incident 5 (same type of information as above)

- Whether or not you addressed the issue by talking to the person indicated and how the discussion went

Feel free to add whatever columns you might feel are needed here—every company is different, and every situation poses different risks and questions, so it is quite important for you to track this the best way for your particular case(s).

Don't add everyone to the spreadsheet. Start with the benefit of the doubt first and only add people who present signs of negative behaviour when you make the realisation.

Also, keep in mind that it is *extremely* important to keep this information secure. Keep it on your computer, not on any kind of cloud storage. Add passwords to your computer and to the file itself and make sure nobody finds them. This is just as important and confidential as wages and salaries—and you wouldn't make those public, right?

This last step is hugely important because it will allow you to make a case when and if the time comes. It will also allow you to shed any doubt over your own judgement, as well, because, yes, trying to be as objective as possible is essential.

Getting your head out of the sand might feel difficult, and it might scare you, especially when you have to deal with people whose negative behaviour goes beyond basic mistakes. However, it is something that is literally the essence of your role and responsibilities as a manager.

Do it now! Don't postpone it any longer!

Thinking Time

Of all the steps described in this chapter, the paper trail is one of the most important ones. Take some time to visualize how your paper trail would look based on the information you have gathered in this chapter and based on your current experience with your employees/team members.

What do you think would be the best way to track the incidents in a way that is compelling, comprehensive, and easy to manage?

Summary

Humans don't naturally like putting themselves into uncomfortable situations, and talking to someone who has been displaying bad behaviour is just that: it puts you (and potentially the person in question, depending on their typology) in a very uncomfortable situation.

Going through all the steps described in this chapter is essential because it will provide you with a solid background on *why* action *must* be taken sooner, rather than later. From the moment you start noticing someone's bad behaviour (or simply from the moment it is brought to your attention by another member of the team) to the moment you have the actual meeting, you will have to make sure you are fully dedicated to making things happen.

At this point, you want to maintain a positive outlook.

Most people can change, unless their behaviour is so bad that they don't even want to see the mistake they are making and unless they really don't care about the repercussions of their actions. Look at the meeting ahead of you as a way to help someone be better and achieve their full potential, rather than a meeting that will inadvertently bring with it a termination of the contract!

Chapter 3

Control Yourself–Managing Your Emotions

Sometimes, being a manager feels like you have to carry the weight of the world on your shoulders because, aside from being responsible for the efficiency of the projects you manage, you are also responsible for the people you manage.

On paper, projects and tasks can look really good when you plan them out. You know what needs to be done, by when, and within what budget. So you just start splitting tasks, assigning them, and planning them.

Unfortunately, however, there are a lot of things that can go wrong, no matter how much you plan. And one of the things that can go wrong is, well, the people you manage.

As I was saying before, your team members are first and foremost *humans*, so they are prone to making mistakes that can delay the project or even damage its quality. That's OK; most things can be fixed. But when one mistake turns into a habit, you have to deal with a negative behaviour already—and that is an entirely different affair.

Dealing with difficult people can be a true challenge, even for the most experienced manager, and from a number of points of view. To begin with, you have to employ the right strategy to make those people turn around and change their behaviours. And that is quite difficult on its own. When you add the fact that you too are human and you are prone to biases, everything can become challenging in the fullest sense of the word.

The way you approach and handle situations is a true integral part of how things will go when dealing with difficult people. Therefore, I have dedicated an entire chapter of this book to help you fix problems you might have yourself, before you dive deep into trying to fix your employees' or your team members' behaviour.

Let's roll this out step by step!

Managing Your Bias

No matter how objective you try to be, you will always be biased, and that happens because you are human and it is only natural to have an opinion about the people around you. Yes, that includes employees, too.

You may like some of them as people, and you may not

like others. That's OK, it's natural. But you should never allow this bias to control how you manage your people, and that is one rule you should never, ever break.

For instance, you may actually like hanging out with Sally, but when Sally is late to work 45 minutes every day, it is time to step in and take action.

Likewise, you may not like John's overall personality (perhaps you dislike his passion for soccer and his habit of betting all his paycheck on soccer games). However, when he is sick a lot of days every month, you should still be able to listen to his side of the story, and you should still be able to see the medical proof he brings in with a clear mind.

In general, you *have to* be able to control your bias and listen to people when you discuss their bad behaviours. Sometimes, there are real issues that make them the way they are, so you should have an open mind whenever you *have the talk* to someone who has been displaying negative behaviour. It is of the utmost importance that you don't allow your own internal monologue to get too negative—or too positive, for that matter.

To control your bias, you should first know what types of biases you might be prone to. Here are some of the biases you might have to fight off (Benson, 2016):

1. Having to deal with way too much information. Don't get this wrong: information is good, and

you should definitely build the foundation of your argument on proper information (which you can gather as described in the previous chapter of this book).

This bias is not as much about the information you document as it is about the information your brain documents. In other words, your brain is wired to notice information that confirms an already existing opinion. For instance, if you think Jack is slacking off, you will definitely notice him doing this on a day when he simply doesn't have much work to do, and you will be drawn to the negative conclusion. Even more, you might not see the other days when Jack does overtime to make sure he over-delivers.

2. Having to deal with insufficient meaning. Unfortunately, our brains are not perfect in the way they reconstruct the puzzle of a story. That means that sometimes, it may have to employ unorthodox techniques to create the story of a bad behaviour. You may have one or two pieces of the puzzle, and your brain will automatically use past information, as well as the stereotypes embedded in your memory to reconstruct the whole story and give you what *seems* to be the full story.

Fighting this bias is all about keeping your mind open and talking to the respective person to actually *listen* to their story. You can't overlap proper meaning on what is happening unless you hear out what that person has to say. Just think of it: even people accused of very serious crimes are given the benefit of the doubt and the right to say their story in court.

3. Having to deal with things *fast*. Everything moves fast. Your car is faster than 100 years ago, your Internet is the fastest way to information (and entertainment), your customers themselves are more impatient, and they want things done *faster*.

Everything is on fast-forward. Which is great for a million reasons, but not that great when you consider the fact that you are human and you have to deal with speeds way beyond your capabilities.

When you feel constrained by time, you are more likely to make rash decisions, which creates a bias in itself. It is very important to apply your information to the given situation and *not* make a rash decision when it comes to an employee. After all, you are dealing with someone's life. So try to find a balance between the need to act fast and not making rash decisions.

4. Having to deal with filtering situations. Your brain is not wired to remember everything. Instead, it makes quick calculations on what it should remember and what it should forget. As a consequence, you may sometimes be biased to

> remember just the big chunks of information and forget the details.

When dealing with negative people, this can turn into a huge bias because you will be more likely to filter out all the great things an employee has done for the company. Or you might be more tempted to filter out the fact that every time Mike is late, he comes to work unshaven and emotionally shattered. He has to make constant phone calls back home to see if his wife is OK. And he has been working two jobs to pay her medical bills.

All of these biases are terribly sad, but that's just the way we have been wired by nature to be able to survive and evolve back when were were just getting out of the trenches. The great news is that you do have the power to fight off these biases and try to acquire a point of view that is as objective as possible. It may not be 100% objective because not even the smartest Artificial Intelligence can do that (they are biased to their programming, which in its own turn is a bias of the team of programmers). But even so, you can get close to no bias—and it's a happy place to aim for.

The whole point of this is that you should *listen* and not just see. When you have a talk to an employee who has been performing badly or had a poor approach to work ethics, *listen*. Communication is a two-way game, just like tennis is. The ball will be on your side of the net, and then on the other person's side until you both reach a common agreement.

The Zero Tolerance approach is not in any way about running over people and keeping to your own, preconceived point of view. It's not "my way or the highway." It's about trying to be as objective as you can and making Zero Tolerance decisions in terms of the second chances you offer, as well as how those are applied.

Controlling Your Emotions

I said this before, but it's so basic that I'll say it again: you and I and all of the employees and team members we handle are all *human*. So we are flawed by the way nature has endowed us with skills and capabilities.

Even more, we are flawed by the emotions our brain releases out in the world. Of course, you shouldn't reprimand your emotions altogether. They are amongst the most amazing reasons that make being human worth it.

However, when dealing with difficult people, it is of the utmost importance that you stay as level-headed as you can. It can be difficult, especially when you have to deal with Rebels, for example, who are always keen on undermining your authority, or with a Manipulator ready to paint you as unprofessional to the rest of the team.

In these situations, your natural reaction would be to match the same level of negativity, and this is not your fault. As mentioned before, this is just how humans are wired, and it's one of the things that has helped us become more resilient and eventually reach the top of the food chain.

The good news (because there always *is* good news to these things) is that you can control most of your emotions. According to an interview with Dr. Brett Ford of the University of Toronto (Pogosyan, 2018), the way we *think* about our emotions has a great influence on how we (should) manage them.

What does this mean?

In a nutshell, it means that some emotions are harder to manage than others. For instance, you will be able to control your facial expressions and tone of voice when dealing with a Rebel, but you may not be able to control the physical response of fear when you are confronted with a burglar in your house.

That is actually good for your body and for your brain. Repressing all emotions has been proven to be unhealthy for a long list of reasons, such as, not being able to cope with grief properly.

At the same time, controlling your emotions at the

correct moments (such as when dealing with difficult people) is the best route to take, especially since allowing your own negativity to take over will lead to nothing good.

The way you perceive your emotions and your beliefs about them influence how you display them—and maybe even more importantly, they influence how you can control them. The more balanced your beliefs are, the more positive you can keep yourself.

How to actually control your emotions (when this is the right way to proceed)? Here are some tips:

1. Change your mindset. A negative mindset is where negative thoughts and emotions are born. So it is extremely important to make sure your mindset is in the right place. Don't look at this situation as one where the person in front of you may retaliate (verbally or, worse, physically, if you have to deal with a particularly bad behaviour). Look at this situation as a chance to get things right by listening to the other person's story, by creating a rehabilitation plan, or, eventually, by re-establishing order within your team.

2. Study your responses to defeat them. If you want to fight an enemy, you must know it as well as you can. The same way goes for emotions, too. Knowing exactly what each emotion represents,

how you respond to it, and how it affects you will help you control it. For instance, if you always rub your hands when you are very nervous, you can spot this habit and remove it when you have to discuss with someone who causes trouble in your team. This will exhibit self-confidence and strength.

In general, there are two types of reactions: reactive and proactive. There is a key distinction between them, and this is something you really need to focus on. A reactive approach means allowing a spur-of-the-moment response to be seen (such as a knee-jerk when you have a discussion with someone problematic in your team). Reactive responses are all about reacting to what people are doing instead of being objective and analytical.

A proactive response, on the other hand, is all about staying on top of the situation—being balanced, acquiring an objective point of view, and staying true to facts. In these cases, you are proactively assessing the situation as it develops in front of you and quickly constructing a correct approach.

3. Focus on what is going well. Even the worst discussions have something good in them. When you are in the middle of the *talk*, consciously shift your attention from whatever is not going well to the things that are going well (e.g., the person in front of you may actually show signs of remorse).

All in all, controlling your emotions is something you should approach in a balanced way. You want to make sure you use this only when it is necessary, such as when dealing with difficult people in the workplace. But outside of these situations, do let your emotions *be*. Shoving them to the depths of your mind will only lead to frustration and bitterness, eventually.

Management Styles: X vs. Y

This might sound like a mathematical chart at best and an X-men movie at its worst, but it's a theory you should definitely keep in mind when addressing this kind of situation.

This is one of the most compelling management theories I have ever stumbled upon, in all my years of perfecting my own management style. Theory X and Theory Y are two management styles developed by Douglas McGregor in the 1960s, in a book called *The Human Side of Enterprise*.

It cannot be said that Theory X is worse than Theory Y or the other way around—they both need to be employed in different situations. Sometimes the first is more effective, while other times the latter is more effective.

The Theory X management style starts with the assumption that humans are lazy by nature. Therefore, they will only work if someone tells them to do so. If nobody tells them to get back to work on a break, they won't do it. Basically, there will always have to be an external source pushing people (back) into work.

The Theory Y management style, on the other hand, focuses on the fact that people actually care about doing meaningful work and feel more worthy as a result. If the work people do fulfills them on various levels (financial, emotional, lifestyle, beliefs, etc.), they will do a good job because it genuinely matters to them.

Whether you should employ Theory X or Theory Y in your management depends a lot on the type of work you do. For instance, if the work performed at your workplace is tedious and not very exciting, employees might feel more tempted to slack off. In this case, Theory X management should be applied.

If you don't want to apply Theory X management style (which you probably don't, because it involves a lot of frustration on all involved sides), you might want to consider changing the value proposition. If you add value to the work people do, they might be far more likely to do it without having to be pushed from behind.

For instance, rubbish collectors might find a lot more value in what they do if they are inspired with the idea that they are doing it for public health and safety, or for the environment (which they are, but someone needs to present this to them).

Another important thing to remember about the Theory X management style is that in general, it is not desirable, because it creates a bad work environment. Ideally, you want to avoid hiring people who cannot be managed otherwise. But, at the same time, it is important for you to acknowledge that if your pay is low and if your company's prestige is low, you might end up hiring this type of people.

Last, but definitely not least, it is crucial for your entire business to apply the right management style for the type of employees you have. Micro-managing someone who is actually motivated will eventually lead them to resign, but not micr0-managing someone who is not motivated will only enable them to slack off.

Thinking Time

Managing your own bias is essential for the well-being of your team and business—this is obvious. Just think of it for a moment: have you ever misjudged an employee? What do you think might have happened if you approached the situation with a more open mind?

Can you think of what approaches you have used to

address negative behaviours in the past? Were you reactive or proactive in your response(s)?

Thinking of all these things might help you find the right balance between controlling your bias and not allowing yourself to be blinded by it. As it has been shown throughout this entire chapter, there are many types of biases, but the good news is that most of the time, they can be controlled to an extent—enough to provide you with a healthier point of view on your employees, their behaviour, and how you need to address it.

Summary

As a manager, you simply cannot allow yourself to be controlled by your emotions, much less when dealing with a difficult employee. At its best, the situation would be a complete waste of time. At its worst, the entire discussion could backfire on you at the speed of light. The person displaying bad behaviour may use your anger or emotions against you, either by badmouthing you to the other members of the team or, maybe worse, by escalating the situation to something much worse.

Most emotions can be controlled. Some cannot and should not (such as grief, for example, when you lose someone dear to you), precisely because emotions exist as a mechanism to protect us from things much darker and much worse than a tear shed or a shout.

However, when it comes to dealing with negative employees, it is of the utmost importance that you restrain all emotions. You must take a professional stance on this and this is completely incompatible with, for example, getting angry at one of your employees (no matter how bad he/she may be).

Biases are a bit different than emotions because they are actually constructed in your brain. Most of the time, they happen involuntarily, because you are wired to create stereotypes and biases to allow you to filter information and memorise only the things your brain thinks are necessary.

The good news is that biases are far more controllable than emotions, and, as with emotions, they are crucial to be contained. Even the smallest bias can make you see someone the wrong way. So it is vital that you remove it altogether and enter *the talk* on a clean slate, with an open mind. If people condemned for terrible acts get a chance to be judged as innocent, a bad employee should get the same chance too.

Chapter 4

The Big Talk–Confronting the Issue

Once you have identified the problem, once you have gotten your bias under control, and once you have learned to control your emotions, you will be able to operate in a factual and objective mindset.

Now it's time to take the Zero Tolerance action and tackle the problem head-on.

The main challenge you may face here is that *talking* and *reading* about being Zero Tolerant might look easy, but confronting the issue might not be that easy. In fact, it might be downright scary if you don't have a lot of experience in dealing with this type of thing, or if you have to deal with employees whose reaction might not be that great.

Zero Tolerance draws its roots in criminal law enforcement. But it is of the utmost importance to understand that this does not make you, the manager, some sort of policeman in the workplace. Taking a balanced approach is the best course of action for you.

Before you jump into action, I also suggest that you take some time to research the employment legislation in your state. Every country and every state has different laws regarding what the employee's rights are, as well as what a manager can or cannot do, under what circumstances, and providing what type of proof.

Why is this essential?

Because you don't want your discussion with a difficult employee to backfire on you and your company. For instance, in some parts of the world, you will learn that employees cannot be fired unless they make very grave mistakes. In these situations, you cannot let go of someone without having them sign their resignation—and in some cases, that might be harder than it looks. There are always escape routes when it comes to this type of situation, but in order to know them, you must first know the legislation where you live and work.

The Zero Tolerance Steps

By now, you should be familiar with some of the theory of how Zero Tolerance works and the essential tips of information you should know about it. Let's pull it all together in a series of actionable steps for you to keep in mind and apply when necessary:

1. Document the mistakes and mishaps. This is very important because it will help you make a case by providing factual data rather than ambiguous references. DO keep in mind that you should not document everyone, every step of the way. But if you start to notice red flags of a bad behaviour, you should definitely start a "file" for that person.

2. Identify the precise repercussions of the bad employee's actions. It might be connected to performance, or you might have to collect circumstantial evidence and witness statements from people who have been affected by it.

3. Take another close look at the legislation you are facing, as well as your company's main policies and procedures. This will help you explain how a certain behaviour goes against your policies, or, in the worst case scenarios, against the legislation itself.

4. Get in the right mindset. We have discussed before how a wrong bias can turn your entire discussion upside-down and how it can do more harm than good. Keep your biases and your emotions under control and embrace a mindset of balance and open-mindedness. This can make ALL the difference in the world!

5. Set a time for discussion with your employee.

There are several factors that will make this go smoother (or at least help you avoid unwanted nightmare scenarios):

- Do it in a private, controlled space - you don't want everyone else to hear what you are talking about with this person, and for a million reasons (including the fact that whatever they might tell you is confidential).

- Bring all your evidence with you and be sure you cross all the T's and dot all the I's when it comes to relaying the information to the employee in front of you.

- Stay calm and collected. You want the person at fault to feel that you are empowered, strong, and not scared of them or the situation.

- ALWAYS judge the behaviour, not the person. It might sound odd, but some people are absolutely amazing in terms of personality, and they turn out to be terrible employees in terms of attitude and behaviour. The vice-versa is true as well: some people are not very pleasant in terms of personality, but they actually do their job well.

6. Explain why the behaviour you are addressing is not fair towards you, towards the other members of the team, or towards the company itself. Bring evidence and witness statements to support your argument—but do make sure you are in control of the situation at all times by not allowing emotions to run you over. Also be careful to protect the information you reference from other employees. Avoid attaching names to statements or reactions.

7. Try to find the reason. Nothing in this world happens without a cause, and your employee's negative behaviour makes no exception to this rule. Now, there is an important distinction to make here. Sometimes people have very real reasons they act the way they do (e.g., they have been working two jobs to support the family and this is why they are late to work). Other times, the cause of their bad behaviour lies much deeper: they might be frustrated, they might have had a bad childhood, they might simply not like you any way you put it.

Whatever it is, try to draw out this root cause underlying their negative behaviour. Doing this will help you create a plausible plan, as well as help you settle realistic expectations (for yourself and for your employee, as well).

8. Create a plan *together*. It is very important that the "rehabilitation" plan you create is done in collaboration with the employee in front of you. This is crucial because it will keep them engaged as well. Some things to keep in mind about this plan are:

- It should be feasible. For instance, if John has been working two jobs and this made him late to work, you cannot expect him to quit the other job, and he cannot expect you to pay double. So, try to find a work schedule that works with him, with you, and with the other members of the crew.

- The expectations should be clear. Don't be ambiguous about it, saying, for instance, "I don't want you to be late again." Instead, tell the person that you want them to be at work at a very specific time of the day, every day from now on. It's also helpful if you can attach a "why" to this so it doesn't sound completely arbitrary.

- The repercussions should be clear as well. Giving people a chance to make things right is one thing, but giving them an indefinite amount of time to make amends is a different one. Be very clear about the changes you want to see, the deadline you give the employee to make these changes, and, ultimately, what happens if sufficient change does not come about.

9. Offer your support. Show your employee that you really want them to succeed and thus that you want to give them all the support they need to make the change happen. Be honest and truthful about this. No matter how badly some people behave, they might actually appreciate the support.

10. Monitor and follow up. This entire discussion will have no meaning if you cannot actually monitor the progress, and then follow up. As you have done throughout the process, try to keep your bias and your emotions under control, even when you see that nothing is changing. Keep in mind the following things:

    - Use the same methodology as you used in the beginning

    - Be consistent

    - If you feel it's needed, set up reminders

on what to watch out for, when to do it, and so on. The life of a manager can get quite hectic, but it is important not to leave this follow up for last.

In all honesty, this is most likely not going to be easy, no matter how you look at it. However, the great news is that sometimes this talk can actually lead to change, and it is much better for everyone when someone changes their bad behaviour than when you see yourself forced to let them go!

Don't look at this discussion as potential material for your nightmares over the next six months. Look at it as a way to give people a second chance. Everyone deserves it, and not even the worst employee in your team is an exception.

Try to keep things as positive as possible. Staying negative and poisoning the entire discussion with your own negative thoughts might actually produce even worse behaviour. So try to keep things optimistic.

What Not to Do?

There are some things you shouldn't do when having the big talk with a negative employee. Some of the most important ones include the following:

1. Don't badmouth employees or spread gossip about them. This is unprofessional at best and actually mean at worst. Keep your discussion with them *private and confidential* in every single respect. There is no reason for anyone on your team to find out what you discussed with the negative employee. Not only is this not ethical and professional, but it poses too great a risk, as the person in question might perceive it as a signal for battle and retaliate.

2. Do not confront or embarrass that person in front of the other team members, or, worse, your clients. This does not say anything good about you and, again, it can lead to a true shouting match between you and said employee (especially if they are usually more abrasive or manipulative).

3. Don't be unprepared. The second the person in front of you sniffs out your unpreparedness is the moment any potentially positive outcome of this discussion will die an abrupt and painful death.

SBR vs. BFE

Dan McCarthy from the University of New Hampshire

(2018), defines two main ways to approach the *problem* when talking to a bad employee:

- SBR: Situation, Behavior, Result
- BFE: Behavior, Feeling, Effect

Although they are very similar, the two approaches pose refined differences which you should be aware of.

Basically, what McCarthy says about dealing with difficult people in the workplace is that when you have the talk, you must follow one of the aforementioned approaches.

SBR focuses on the direct impact a behaviour might have:

1. Explain the situation (e.g., "I saw you come 50 minutes late to work this Wednesday").

2. Explain why this is a habitual behaviour (e.g., "It is not the first time I have seen you come to work so late.").

3. Explain the response (e.g., "And this might actually affect the other members of your team because they will not see this to be fair.").

BFE, on the other hand, focuses on what a behaviour can make someone *feel* like:

1. Behaviour (e.g., "When I saw you come late to

work for the third time in a row...")

2. Feeling (e.g., "..., I felt like the other members of this team and I are not important to you.")

3. Effect (e.g., "This sets a poor example for everyone else on the team.").

These patterns will help you initiate conversation with the troubled employee without making them feel like they are completely put to the wall (and thus, without making them too defensive).

Thinking Time

Every manager has his own way of approaching things. The management style he/she employs, the situation he/she has to face, and the personality he/she embraces will all influence the way he/she approaches unwanted situations.

What approach do you think would be best for you, if you had to choose between SBR and BFE? Have you used any of these in the past, and if so, why? What could have gone better?

Consider these matters when choosing which pattern you should use. The right wording can, indeed, make a huge difference in how your negative employee perceives this entire discussion.

Summary

Taking the bull by its horns is not only the best way to tackle a difficult person in your workplace—it is *the only way*.

Postponing this will only allow the negative behaviour to grow and potentially spread to other employees as well. And, before you know it, you might have to deal with an epidemic of people late to work, people who complain about everything, or people who simply slack off the whole day long.

If you have never done this before, and particularly if your bad employee is *extremely bad* (e.g., he/she is constantly undermining authority in the worst of ways), having this discussion will be even more uncomfortable than normal.

However, there is no way you can escape it. Without this discussion, you cannot help change the vibe of your workplace—either by correcting the bad team member or, eventually, by terminating his/her contract.

Even more, if termination has to be applied, you will find that this discussion will help you set the foundation stone of your paper trail, precisely because in most cases you will need documentation to support your decision to let someone go (both in front of them and in front of the authorities).

No matter how you look at the matter, the issue must be confronted, and avoiding it will only make things worse.

Chapter 5

The Road Ahead–Making Progress

The Zero Tolerance approach is not in any way about making swift, irreversible decisions. It is about enforcing a system where progress and change are not only allowed, but encouraged.

Simply having a discussion with an employee who displays negative behaviour is, sadly, not enough. And while I definitely know you have a lot on your hands and that you have to handle an entire team, it is important to know that planning and monitoring the progress of your employee is just as important as planning and monitoring the progress of your business.

Why?

Because one employee can drive a business into the ground if the behaviour is negative enough.

But a good employee can actually push your business further.

When it comes to teams, quantity does not always determine the extent to which they can affect a business. It's all a matter of quality—the quality of what each and every single employee in your business does.

If you want to correct bad behaviours and enforce the "good" Zero Tolerance method, you must put a lot of emphasis on *progress*—just as much as you have been putting into developing the background of your big talk with the bad employee.

The chapter at hand is dedicated to helping you do this. The more thorough you are in your monitoring, the more successful the entire endeavour can be.

Observe and Note Progress

As mentioned before, this stage is just as important as the preparations themselves are and just as important as any other part of the entire process.

You can either create separate documentation for the monitoring of progress, or you can add it as a continuation of your initial observations. In truth, both options are just as good, as long as you stick to them and as long as you are consistent and persevering.

Just because you had a talk to someone, no matter how serious and how clear it might have been, it doesn't actually mean that they will start applying the directives you gave.

When you note down the progress a person makes towards redemption, do keep in mind the following:

- Are they *trying* to make an effort at least? Even if they don't actually manage to do *everything* right and change their behaviour a full 180 degrees, the effort should count for something. It means that they still want to stay with your team, and it means that they might actually regret their behaviour.

- Are they succeeding, but with difficulty? Changing one's behaviour is not easy. Just think of it: if you eat poorly every single day, taking in fast food and candy all day long, every day, for weeks, months, and even years in a row, leaving this kind of behaviour behind will be difficult. The same goes for an employee who displays a bad behaviour. If they are succeeding at your prescribed changes, but you see them continue to struggle, it's a sign that there is still much work to do. It is also a sign that they are trying very hard, which might actually turn into a positive aspect along the way, but it can foreshadow a relapse, as well.

- Do they need further guidance and support? It is

of the utmost importance that you offer your genuine support when it comes to correcting someone's bad behaviour. Do make sure your support is genuine, continuous, and that you emphasise it a lot.

You need to keep a close eye on someone who has been displaying bad behaviour and make sure they do not forget about the discussion you had. Do this in a positive way, and be there to help and support. Sometimes, it can make such a huge difference in how the bad employee perceives the whole situation that they might even start working harder as a sign of respect for what you are doing.

Sure, this is not always the case, and some people are just *too* negative for redemption. However, offering everyone a chance to correct their bad behaviours is important because it sends out a powerful signal, to the offending employee and to the other members of the team, as well.

Behaviours to Avoid

As a manager handling a difficult employee, you cannot allow yourself to slip into bad behaviours yourself. It will make everyone lose trust in your actions and words, and it can lead to further negativity as well.

This is why it is extremely crucial that you stay away from some of the most common bad behaviours managers display in these types of situations:

- Lack of consistency. If you simply measure the progress of an employee for one week, then skip another, and then remember to start measuring their progress towards the end of the trial period, you will eventually end up with inconsistent results—information you cannot actually draw a proper conclusion on. And yes, proper data and witness statements are just as important now as they were when you were first monitoring the employee before you had an actual discussion with them!

- Employee favouritism. As I mentioned in a previous chapter, biases are not always negative. Sometimes, you might spend quality time with a team member outside of the workplace. They might live near you, they might be in your circle of common friends, or they might even be related to you. These are circumstances that you need to treat with a high level of caution.

Even more, you may simply like the personality of a person who is displaying bad behaviour—for instance, someone who is always late might also be extremely funny, and they might cheer up the ones around them by bringing cookies and cake to work every Monday.

This does not excuse the fact that they are stealing company time, though, and especially on a recurrent basis. Avoid employee favouritism at all costs, no matter what the motivation behind it might be. It is really, really important to stay objective and judge the behaviour, not the person!

- Gossiping. Badmouthing your team members to other team members says something really nasty about you: it says that you are not professional, it says that you are a bit of a Manipulator yourself, and it says that you cannot keep the confidence of a discussion as sensitive as the one you had.

Avoid gossiping, even when you are challenged and indirectly encouraged to do it. Keep a professional, ethical stance on this: your employee deserves a full second chance in every respect. Badmouthing them will either make them lose self-confidence in the redemption acts they are pursuing *or* it will make them become resilient, reactive, and potentially aggressive, willing to pay you with the same coin.

Practice what you preach. Nobody will find a gossiping manager credible when the behaviour he/she is trying to correct in an employee is gossiping itself (or even when the employee's bad behaviour is miles away from that).

You simply cannot tell everyone to stay positive when you are filled with negativity yourself. And you most definitely cannot tell people to show up on time when you are late one hour every day, when everyone sees you scrolling your Facebook page 28 times a day, and when you "shy" away from daily tasks by simply faking work.

A leader is much more than a *boss*. A leader is someone who works alongside their team, someone who helps and supports them, someone who inspires them, someone who mentors them.

This is the same as going to a cardiologist who smells like cigarettes. Would you find them credible, inspiring, or in any way qualified to give advice on your health? Probably not as much. Their credentials and studies recommend them for this kind of job and the kind of advice they give, but their own behaviour might cast a shadow of doubt on their credibility.

You need to set an example. And yes, this means showing up to work every day on time, it means staying positive, it means never slacking off, never badmouthing anyone, and never trying to scheme your way into making people believe you are very busy. And yes, this means you should do all these things even if you are the owner of the company.

Not doing it will not only make your employees or team members lack motivation. It will actually set a bad example and it will eventually make everyone feel frustrated, sad, and completely out of touch with what they do.

Learn How to Give Negative Feedback

When applying the Zero Tolerance approach, you might sometimes find yourself in the situation of giving bad feedback. This is important, even though it might not be very pleasant (for you or for your employee).

It is crucial that you constantly monitor and provide feedback to someone who is under observation, and not just give them feedback at the end of the trial period. This will allow them to make progress based on the adjustments you suggest, and it will allow you to have a better, more comprehensive view of things.

Giving negative feedback can be extremely tricky because the main point behind it is to be constructive, but when handled the wrong way, it can turn into a negative experience itself. Framing a critique correctly and in a constructive way is not an ability most people are *born* with; it is a skill you need to learn, practice, and master. It is a skill that is related to proper communication, as much as it is related to management techniques and psychology.

Some of the most important tips to keep in mind here include:

1. Managing your emotions. We have already covered this in our previous chapters, but we

need to emphasise it here again because it is just as important when giving feedback. When you critique someone while angry or upset, your message can come out very wrong, even if you control the actual words.

2. If the situation gets out of control and you or your employee grow angry, place the discussion on hold and reschedule it for the next day. It is far better to proceed this way than continue a discussion that could deviate into actual aggression (verbal or otherwise).

3. Don't leave too much time to pass between the incident and your feedback. The more time you leave, the less likely it is that the person in front of you will follow your feedback.

4. Don't deliver negative feedback in front of the person's peers. It will make them feel self-conscious, embarrassed, and/or rejected. As a consequence, it will automatically drive them in the direction of self-defence and aggression. Even more, it will make them feel much less keen on actually hearing out what you have to say.

5. Be concise, clear, and specific. Simply telling someone that they have not improved their behaviour or that they didn't do good is not enough. Be very specific about the incident, what

went wrong, and how you would like to see the employee improve. Even more, be very specific about the repercussions of their actions—they need to know *why* what they are doing is wrong.

For instance, someone may not see it *that* wrong that they are late to work every day for 20 minutes, but when you explain that 20 minutes every day for a week equals approximately one and a half hours and that it leads to an almost entire day of work lost in one month, they might understand the issue better. Even more, if you tell them that their actions have repercussions on their colleagues, they might feel more compelled to take action against their bad behaviour.

6. Be specific about the results you are expecting, as well. You can't expect someone to reach a goal if you don't tell them that goal. That would be the same as evaluating an employee's performance over a given period of time and telling them they have not reached their KPIs when those indicators had never been relayed to them.

7. Be polite. Seriously, the right words (*please, thank you,* and *you're welcome*) can make all the difference in the world. They can actually make the difference between a "horrible boss" and a *leader*.

8. Don't give orders. That's not what true leaders

do. Instead, give advice and counsel. Show people they are wrong by relying on facts and good wording. "Stop being late, Sam!" sounds *a lot* worse than "Sam, I have noticed that you continue to be late at work. This causes losses for the business, and it puts a lot of stress on your workmates, who have to work overtime to cover for your lateness. I know you have had issues, but I would very much like it if I saw you make progress towards resolving those issues. I have all my faith in you because I know what a great programmer you are!" Giving orders is not a good way to give feedback (it defeats the very purpose of constructive feedback). However, do keep in mind that sometimes, orders are necessary —*only* when it pertains to the health and safety of the team members.

9. Take it in a positive direction. There is a reason you hired this person in the first place. They might actually be skilled and talented, for example. Don't forget to tell them you still have faith in them, in their abilities, and more importantly, in their capacity to overcome this situation and become the best version of themselves. Furthermore, if the employee has been making progress (albeit not enough), be sure to reinforce their success and thank them for their hard work. It is extremely important to

recognize when someone does a good job, even when they are on "trial."

10. Remember that communication is a two-way act. Once you have relayed your feedback, be sure you encourage the other person to speak as well. They might give an explanation, or they might simply promise you to do better. If you have to deal with a particularly bad employee, they might still get defensive, no matter how much you try to avoid it, so be prepared. Furthermore, encourage the employee or team member to give their input, as well. What do they think should be done for them to correct their behaviour? Sometimes, they can find the answers themselves—and when the solution comes from their own thought process, they are far more likely to pursue it and succeed.

Do consider the fact that sometimes, no matter how much you try and no matter how great your feedback is, people are resilient to change. It is, again, something that has been built into our DNA. We like comfort. We like being the way we are now. Change means effort, and effort is not something most people actually aim for.

Therefore, you should prepare for cases when difficult employees simply refuse to take any kind of action to fix their behaviour. They might change things for a short amount of time (enough to get out of the muddy waters), and then return to their old behaviour. And other times, people try very hard, but continue to fail.

Acknowledge the fact that having a discussion with a bad employee is not the end of the process. In fact, it is the beginning. Our next chapter is dedicated to teaching you what to do when positive, consistent change fails to occur. Yes, this might happen. And, like it or not, it is your duty as a manager to address this kind of situation, as well.

Thinking Time

Giving feedback and directions the right way can make or break the results of the discussion you are having with a difficult employee.

Stop for a moment and rewind all the moments you have given feedback and directions before. How did you proceed? Is there any way you could have done better?

Chapter 6

What Do You Say—Ultimatums and Check-Ups

Simply having a discussion with a poorly performing or difficult employee is frequently not enough. Pointing out what they have been doing wrong in a way that is constructive, rather than critical is, surely, essential. But so is giving an ultimatum and running regular check-ups. Without a deadline, your difficult employee will most likely not respond to your suggestions. And without your clearly explaining the consequences of doing so or not, they will be even more likely not to follow your advice.

It is what it is—that's the way a lot of people function. Without a clear ultimatum, most people just go about their business and don't mind feedback unless it is relayed in a way that makes it crystal-clear that there will be repercussions.

Even when you do make things clear, some people might

not take it very seriously or they might simply have trouble adapting to your "new" rules. Or they might test you. That is precisely why constant check-ups (meetings that follow the rules of the initial one) are necessary. They will help you reinforce your point of view and remind the bad employee that they are being watched for the negative behaviours they are displaying.

This chapter is all about dealing with those situations when, unfortunately, people do not immediately start to change. This is not to say that they *won't* change under any circumstances, but in order for that to happen, you must address and re-address the issue as often as possible during the "trial" period (the time frame you have given them to apply the feedback you have offered).

I must warn you: this is not going to be easy. It takes hard work to make sure you have given your employee all the tools they need to succeed and to make it extremely clear that you are not joking around.

So, without further ado, let's dive into the steps you need to follow during the check-up period:

1. Set the follow-up meeting. This should be done towards the end of the initial meeting because you will most likely want to speak to the employee again. If they have been improving, be sure to tell them that you have noticed a change in their behaviour and give them further suggestions on how they can do better.

If they haven't done much towards the end goal, be sure you emphasise that time is running short, as well as the importance of doing following through and that you will have to enforce punishment if nothing happens.

The follow-up meeting will be based on the same structure and rules as the initial meeting. However, it will most likely take a completely different direction because the employee sitting in front of you already knows why you are having this meeting and the behaviours that led them there.

If the behaviour has not been corrected (or at least not too much), it is important for you to find out if this happened because it is difficult for the person in front of you or simply because they don't care. There is a huge difference between the two situations: the first can be remedied eventually in most cases. The second, however, points to a typology of employee who simply does not want to do better and cannot be motivated to do it in any other way than by being threatened.

Do keep in mind that, at the end of this meeting, you will also have to update your paper trail. This is just as important as the documentation of every step you make in this entire process.

   2. Do make sure you pay attention to excuse-making. When put in difficult situations, some types of difficult employees will try to manipulate their way out. And one of the most common

ways they do this is by making excuses. Yes, there are valid situations that may prevent them from properly applying your feedback, but in most cases, these situations are rare.

In most of the (other) cases, people are just trying to make excuses. This might get more poignant with some typologies of difficult employees, such as the Manipulator or even the Workplace Thief. These typologies tend to have an endless list of excuses they can turn to whenever their flaws are pointed out—it almost feels like a cartoon episode where the devil is unfolding a mile-long parchment full of excuses, on top of excuses, on top of some more excuses. If the situation weren't very serious and if it didn't have serious consequences, this could be, indeed, comical.

But it isn't, and neither you nor your bad employee should treat it like this in any way. Someone who constantly makes excuses is likely not to improve their behaviour. In fact, they might let it run completely loose. And when that happens, this can seriously affect your entire team and eventually your business.

Yes, as sad as it may be, one bad apple can really ruin the whole basket. This is where it becomes extremely important for you to know the main typologies of problematic employees. Knowing each of them in particular and knowing how to deal with them is of the utmost importance.

3. Set penalties. In some cases, this might have to be at least touched upon in the initial meeting. Otherwise, it will have to be set in stone during the follow-up meeting (provided that the employee shows no signs of change, of course).

It is *crucial* that you set penalties and stick to your word. For instance, if someone is consistently late, you could tell them that you will have to cut their pay for the hours they didn't work. Especially for the employee who is motivated by their finances, you will have an impactful form of leverage at your disposal. But even for someone who is less concerned about their wallet, this sort of tangible, calculable consequence is a stern wakeup call.

Regardless of what penalties you decide to set with the difficult employee, it is really important to follow through with your promise. Not doing so will only make you look weak and it will make it seem as if you aren't dedicated to making the change. Therefore, the difficult team member will not take you seriously.

Enforcing the penalty, however, will help you make it clear to the person what the deal is. If they completely fail by the end of the trial period, it will not come as a surprise to them if you have to enforce the ultimate threat—letting them go. This whole process will also make it easier for you to justify your decision in that case.

Now, it is really important not to think negatively and consider that all your efforts will actually lead in that direction. Some people *do* change their behaviour, so you should start with this presumption. However, you should prepare for the worst, as well.

4. Give an ultimatum, when necessary. Unfortunately, this is many times the only way to make some types of difficult people change their behaviour. You need to be really clear about this: they will either improve before a given deadline or termination (or some other escalating form of discipline) will ensue. As with penalties, it is vital that you follow through with your ultimatum.

Sometimes this is the most efficient way to make people improve themselves. Fear of not having a job is a strong motivator for the vast majority of employees, except for very few cases when they are keen on undermining your authority even if that brings along a termination.

Thinking Time

Setting an ultimatum is never an easy choice. No matter how bad a team member may be, you will still find it difficult to set an ultimatum in stone. And following through may actually break you psychologically because you will probably think of the consequences it will bring for the person and their family.

No, it is not a nice way to end things. But it is absolutely necessary if you want your company to grow, if you want every other team member to feel safe and motivated at work, and if you want things to go well for everyone. It is the hard decision you have to take as a manager—frequently, to the betterment of everyone else.

Stop and think for a moment: Have you ever had to set an ultimatum in the past? Did you stick to your word?

Also, what sorts of excuses have you heard from your employees or team members? What type of Difficult Personality Profile would you apply to them?

Summary

Regardless of what kind of team you may be managing, and regardless of its size, your main purpose as a manager is not in any way to fire people.

Your purpose is to ensure the product (be it a house, a software program, or a doll) is delivered successfully to its customer, to help or entertain that customer, and to create a good experience for them.

In order for that to happen, you need to make sure all the people under your management fall in line—not in an authoritarian way, but in a very democratic and collaborative way.

In every healthy society, people are subjected to a series of duties and rights. In the case of your employee or team members, those duties are all about doing their job correctly.

Their rights are all about being treated fairly. Since the scope of this book is not discrimination in the workplace or another thousand ways employees might be treated unfairly, we will not discuss those situations.

However, when it comes to dealing with difficult employees and, when necessary, terminating their employment, their rights are all about making sure that they have been given a chance to redeem themselves and change their behaviour.

From the moment you have the initial talk to the moment you terminate a contract (if that is the case and *if* you will reach that point), it is important to show (and document!) the fact that you have offered your constant support in the achievement of said goals.

Chapter 7

Failure and Fallout—When to Terminate

As a manager and as a human being, I truly wish you to never reach this stage.

The first time you have to let someone go might feel as if you were tearing a part of your soul into pieces. Doing so, you simply cannot avoid thinking of everything that will change in that person's life, how it will influence every single area, how their families will take it, and, eventually, how everyone else on the team might perceive you.

Unfortunately, this is one of the hardest decisions you will have to make as a manager. Sometimes, it might feel easier to decide what to do with millions of dollars than to decide what to do with one employee.

Termination is never something you want to think of. Not as an employee, nor as a manager.

No matter how much we dislike it, though, it is sometimes the *only* viable option. You cannot keep someone around who is consistently late, who doesn't listen to anything in the meetings, who fails to deliver KPIs consistently, who undermines your authority in the worst of ways, or who badmouths everyone around them, making your workplace feel extremely negative for everyone there.

You might try to convince yourself that they will not have that noticeable an influence on everyone else. But in my experience, negativity spreads like the plague, and it can turn around even the most loyal and hardworking employees. It is how groups of people work—we tend to do what our neighbours do.

The Sociology of Groups

This might seem like it doesn't have much room in the discussion here, but it's everything that matters, really.

The reason *one* employee can ruin it all for everyone else is because that is how the sociology of group behaviour works. Negative behaviour can really catch on like the plague, and this comparison is not an exaggeration of any kind.

Almost every language in the world has a saying that traces back to how we are more inclined to mimic the behaviour of the groups we identify with. In English, that is *keeping up with the Joneses*. In Spanish, it's *mantenerse al dia con los vecinos* (which translates, word by word, to *keeping it up to date with your neighbours*).

We want to conform to the groups we belong to. Even when those groups are unconventional (e.g., you are a heavy metal rocker), you still conform to the behaviours and attributes established by the group.

Your team is, at its foundation, a social group. They spend at least eight hours together every day, and eventually they will influence each other's behaviour. The easiest way to notice this is how some of them will pick up expressions others use, even if they didn't use them before.

When they start to pick up bad behaviours, however, this can become troublesome for the entire team, and it can eventually hurt the entire business.

It is said that humans are social animals, and this is largely connected to the idea of groups. Few people are deliberately solitary. Most of us look to our groups and find support in them. Things have been so ever since humans started to evolve. By this point, it is embedded in our deepest DNA.

Groups are essential for social life, and they are essential for social stability itself. Every person in a group has a role to play. Some are leaders (divided, in sociology, in two large groups: authoritarians and democrats). Some are followers. Some are idea makers. Others are doers.

And some are bad apples. This is the kind of role you want to eliminate from a group because it will, sooner or later, influence the other members of that group.

There are two experiments I would like to point out to prove just how essential group dynamics can be.

The first one is that of Solomon Asch and the perception of line lengths (Mcleod, 2018). This experiment was run in the 1950s, but it stands just as vital today. Asch took two cards, one with a line and another one with three lines. He told students that the length of the line on the first card corresponded to the length of one of the lines on the second card.

The answer was quite obvious: line B on the second card corresponded in length with the line on the first card.

However, when some of the students gave a wrong answer, multiple wrong answers followed. When asked why they gave that answer, a large portion of the students simply said they didn't want to be different from the other ones in their group. So, the wrong answer simply carried from one student to another because they all wanted to be like the other members of their group.

Imagine this applied in workplace dynamics. If Sally is late every day, John may start to be late every day, too. And by the end of the year, you will have to face the fact that, in a team of 30, you have lost 30 whole days of work simply because *one* employee was consistently late for 20 minutes.

The second experiment I would like to bring to your attention is even more shocking: Stanley Milgram and the Electric Shock (Mcleod, 2017).

This experiment was conducted at Yale University in the 1970s, and it wanted to answer questions regarding the murdering of millions of people during the Holocaust. In the years following World War II, a lot of people asked themselves *how it was possible* that so many human beings were systematically murdered so close to them. *Where were we* is a leitmotif question that has been running around for decades now.

Stanley Milgram attempted to answer the question with an experiment trying to prove that it wasn't Germans' inclination to submit to authoritarian leadership that was the root of all problems, but the way society functions in itself.

The experiment involved a subject (the "teacher"), who would come into a laboratory and be told by someone dressed in a white lab coat to send electric shocks to another subject (the "learner"). Depending on the type of experiment, the learners were located in three places:

- In another room, and they were heard through a loudspeaker, but they were not seen by the teachers

- In another room, and they were heard through a loudspeaker and seen through a window by the teachers
- In the same room, right next to the teachers.

Whenever a wrong answer was delivered by the learners, the teachers had to send an electric shock to their bodies by pushing a button. The shocks became increasingly more powerful, up to 450 V, which was marked on the machine as *Dangerous*. However, because they were told to do this by an authoritarian figure (the men in white lab coats), the teachers had no problem in enforcing this rule, and some went as far as administering the full-powered shock.

What the teachers didn't know is that the machine they were using was not administering any kind of shock to the learners, as the sounds of pain they were hearing were just recordings. Even so, they had no remorse about inflicting what they thought was pain to someone else, a complete stranger, just because the authority figure told them so.

This is an extreme example, of course.

But think of what happens if the members of your team stop perceiving you as their leader and start perceiving a Manipulator as their leader. Wouldn't that ruin the cohesion of the entire team, and, eventually, the wellbeing of the business itself?

It may seem that neither of these experiments have anything to do with how real life management works. But in truth, they show very well how groups function from a sociological point of view. And chances are that your team is no different from these well-established tendencies.

When to Terminate

Knowing when a second chance has turned into too much for your team and company to take is essential. There are several things you should keep in mind when it comes to terminating an employee, and I will split them in three main sub-sections, each dedicated to an actual stage of the termination. It is important not to skip any of these sections, as they are all vital to the entire process.

When Enough Is Enough

Giving an ultimatum is extremely important, but it is equally important to make sure you actually follow through on your word, as well. You need to boldly enforce your ultimatum.

By this point, you have had an initial formal discussion with your difficult employee, you have created a plan together, you have followed through with feedback again and again, and you have eventually decided to give them an ultimatum. Most of the time, this process can take at least three months (or more, depending on what timeline you decide on). If, by the end of this period, you still see no major improvement in the person's behaviour, the ultimatum must be enforced.

Enough is enough. With all the chances you have already offered this person, it would be hard for anyone (authorities or other employees) to judge your decision as rash. In the end, you have given this person not just *one* second chance, but multiple (if you consider the follow-ups as well). You have offered all your support in helping said person to redeem themselves and correct their behaviour.

Giving them yet another chance will only make it seem that you are weak and that you will never actually terminate. As a consequence, the difficult employee may go about their behaviour, not changing much, and sticking to their old ways.

When all of this has happened, you simply cannot continue to work with this person. It is of the utmost importance that you take the final step.

So let's move on to the next three stages of the termination. The first one (the one we're discussing right now) is actually making the decision to move further. The second one is gathering and putting your paper trail in order. The third one is considering labor laws in your country or state and then taking action.

Do make sure you follow the same timeline you agreed on with your employee during your most recent meeting (the one where you gave them the ultimatum). If you said that you would give them one month, make sure the termination happens no sooner and no later than that.

Moreover, do make sure you prepare yourself psychologically. If this is the first time you are terminating someone's contract, you will find this extremely difficult. And even if you have had similar experiences before, you will still find the situation to be unpleasant (to say the least).

However, please keep in mind that you are doing this for the sake of your entire team and business.

The Paper Trail

This has been emphasised throughout this entire book precisely because of its importance. Keeping a paper trail and proper documentation on the evolution of a difficult employee is important not only because it will help *you* make sense of it all, but also because it will help someone with an outside perspective to make sense of it. Your paper trail will provide you with all the necessary evidence when the termination must be enforced.

You need to make sure you have proper information and that it is properly dated, just in case you need to show it to the employee in question, or, in the more extreme examples, to authorities should they ask questions.

DO make sure you document everything: from the moment you start noticing the bad behaviour, the discussion you have with the employee, the follow-up(s), the ultimatum, and the changes that occur or don't occur. Log times, witness statements, and everything that could help you make your case should be considered as useful evidence.

Furthermore, DO make sure your paper trail is correctly organized, in chronological order: the first incidents you noticed, when, who can attest to this, the logged times you have, and everything that can prove those first incidents. Next, you should add to your documentation the discussion you had with the employee, the conclusions that were drawn, and the agreement you reached with them. The follow-up documentation should be built and organized on the same pattern, and it should be followed by any changes (or lack of changes) that occurred in the behaviour of the person in cause.

Putting your documentation in order represents the first stage of the documentation process. Don't rush through it, and make sure you have all the paperwork you need to make your case.

Labour Laws

This is extremely important to consider. Depending on where you live, not respecting labor laws might attract the authorities upon you and it can eventually cause serious damage to your business (fines, for example). Of course, you want to manage your team with proper ethics anyway.

Labour laws are vastly different around the world. In some countries, they tend to side with employees, trying to protect them from unfair treatment in the workplace. In other countries, however, they are more balanced, and as long as you can provide authorities with evidence, you will be fine.

For instance, in the United States of America, most employees can be fired at will, any time. Even so, there are reasons that are considered to be illegal for the termination of a work contract, such as:

- Discrimination
- Alien status
- Refusing to take a lie detector test
- Complaints related to Occupational Safety and Health Act
- The violation of a public policy

To show *just* how different laws can be, consider the fact that, in the United Kingdom, the employer must give the employee a legal notice. This can amount to one week (if the employee has been working there between one month and two years), or up to twelve weeks (if the employee has been working there for more than two years, with one week added to the minimum legal notice with every year the employee has been working there).

The only reasons considered to be fair for an employer to fire the employee without notice are related to gross misconduct, such as theft, fraud, or violence. Reasons considered to be fair for an employer to fire the employee *with* notice include conduct and behaviour, capability, redundancy, the breaking of a statutory restriction, or other substantial reasons (such as restructuring, for example).

Even when these reasons are legitimate, you must make it official that you have investigated the issue, and that you have held a disciplinary hearing where the employee has the right to challenge the evidence.

This circles back to just how important your paper trail is. Without it, you don't have a case, and you cannot legally terminate a contract (in the UK, at least, and in many other parts of the world, too).

Do check with the labor laws where you live and work, and be very much aware of the fact that sometimes the legislation can be vary even from one state to another. If in doubt, make sure to check with an attorney; it is always better to err on the safe side when it comes to these issues, especially since illegally firing someone can bring serious consequences upon you and your business.

How to Actually Do It

Unfortunately, there is no set recipe to help you go through this easily. There are, however, a bunch of tips you might want to keep in mind when it comes to terminating a contract.

Some of the most important ones include the following:

1. This has been said before, but it really needs to be emphasised: before termination, you should show that you have tried to help the employee improve their behaviour and/or performance.

Writing down every detail in your paper trail, being a genuinely good coach and trying to help said employee change, being very clear about your expectations from them, creating a performance improvement plan (PIP), and, if needed, a written counselling (which is similar to a PIP, but in more detail and in written)—they are all stages that should precede a termination. This is all the more important if you live in a country where such paper trail needs to be brought forward when making your argument to authorities.

2. Hold the meeting somewhere where you won't be bothered. In general, this type of meeting should not last more than 10 to 15 minutes. Anything longer than that is, harsh as it may seem, a waste of time both for you and for your employee.

Most people want more, because they want to give further justification for their actions. However, prolonging the meeting will only make you more likely to come back on your decision. And that is simply an option not to consider. There are a lot of pieces of factual evidence and multiple discussions that have led you to this point. Reconsidering your decision will only make you seem weak and it will reinforce bad behaviour.

3. You won't like this, but the termination announcement has to be swift. Politely greet the person, invite them to come in and sit down, and set the tone of the meeting from the very beginning by telling them you have bad news for them. This is essential because it will not make the employee feel off-guard when the news is delivered, and thus, they will not get as defensive.

State the fact that you are terminating the contract, as well as the reason behind it. If you have gone through all the stages described thus far in the book, the person in front of you knows what this is all about and they know that consistent effort has been shown on your side to

- help them improve.

Be clear about the terms of the termination and use the past tense when you mention this (e.g., say "Your contract has been terminated as of today," instead of "Your contract will be terminated as of today"). This is a psychological technique to help the person in front of you realise that this is already *done* and cannot be undone.

Be specific about the next steps as well: what pay benefits you might have to give, what happens with the unused vacation time, if you can give them references, and so on.

Most likely, the employee will have a series of questions, so you should prepare to answer them right there, on the spot. Some of these questions might include:

- When should the employee leave?

- Is this their last day?

- Will they receive any kind of severance pay? How about the bonuses they were eligible for? And how about their last paycheck—what will it cover and when will it be paid?

- Will they be paid for vacation time not taken?

- Will you be able to provide them with references—and if so, will they be positive?

- When will the medical insurance benefits stop?

- Is there something the employee must return, such as laptops or a work phone?

4. Do not try to justify yourself. If your paper trail is in order and if you have been following the right steps to the moment, the employee should know what this is all about. Explaining the reason is one thing, but trying to justify your actions will only make you look weak.

5. Do not make this a personal attack. This was valid throughout every other meeting and follow-up you had with the difficult employee until now, so it should stand just as true during the final moments. Don't say things like "You had it coming." It will only make the situation worse and it can potentially lead to aggressive moments as well.

6. Remember that this should be a face-to-face meeting. Under no circumstances should it be done on the phone or via email, as it will leave room for interpretation and it will make it even harder for the employee to take the news.

7. Bring in a witness. This is important especially under US legislation, where suing anyone can be extremely easy. Having a witness by your side will help you avoid unwanted situations in the future, coming from an angry (fired) employee.

8. Try to avoid allowing the employee to get back to the work area and colleagues. You want to minimize the contact they have with everyone else—for their own good and to preserve their dignity (since they might be visibly angry) and for the good of the rest of the team as well.

9. Offer to send their belongings to them or to allow them to come and pick them up on a weekend. This will help you subtract any kind of confidential details the employee might be holding about the clients of your company, and it will also help you preserve their dignity.

10. Remove access to the informational system immediately. You should leave *no* time between the moment you fire the employee and the moment you terminate access to the informational system. Even ten minutes can mean they will copy confidential information to a USB stick or to a personal cloud account and use them against you in the future. Yes, that is a possibility, especially with some types of bad employees.

This can never be done the easy way. Psychologically, legally, and even from the point of view of how the rest of the team will perceive the whole situation, terminating an employee is, without doubt, one of the most terrible experiences you have to take responsibility for as a manager. Be sure you do it right, using the proper documentation and not prolonging the agony!

Thinking Time

If you have some experience in management, there is a fair chance that you might have had to go through this type of situation before.

Have you ever had to actually terminate employees in the past? Did you use proper documentation in the process? Even more, did you give a fair warning in advance?

If you didn't, you should 100% make certain you do it in the future!

Summary

Nobody likes thinking of the worst-case scenario. However, when you have already offered all your sustained support in helping someone correct negative behaviour and they fail to deliver any kind of change (or insufficient, at that), it is time to terminate the employment contract.

DO keep in mind the fact that you should NEVER

terminate anyone's employment on illegal grounds (and remember that those are different from one country to another). Check with your attorney or internal HR department to ensure that your reason is founded and that you have all the necessary paper trail to make this happen.

Without a legal reason and without evidence to support your decision, you could be getting yourself and your business into huge trouble. No matter how awful an employee may be, doing this the *fair* and *legal* way is, without doubt, the only way to handle the situation.

Chapter 8

When They're Not Your Employee–Clients, Partners, and Bosses

Negative behaviours are everywhere.

You will meet them on the bus, on your way home. You will meet them in school. You will meet them in the workplace. And you might even have to deal with them in your personal life.

Unfortunately, you cannot change the fact that many people are just negative by nature or that they have grown to be so as a result of external influence.

When it comes to your employees, there is a pretty clear path you can take, and all of it is based on the fact that, as a manager (owner, entrepreneur, etc.), you have the power to do this. You have the authority to call meetings with employees, tell them that they are not doing well, help them improve and, eventually, if that doesn't happen, terminate their contracts.

However, when you don't have the authority to enforce rules, it might be a bit more difficult to handle a difficult situation. For instance, what happens when the negative behaviour in your workplace comes from a partner, a client, or your boss?

Clearly, you cannot simply call for a meeting and threaten to terminate your collaboration with them. Doing this with a partner or a client can inflict irreparable damage on your business, and doing this with your own boss can lead to very unhealthy (and potentially career-threatening) situations.

This chapter is dedicated to helping you deal with difficult people that are not your team members or employees. The situation can be even more delicate than everything described thus far in this book, but the great news is that there *are* things you can do.

Let's dive in!

When Your Client Is Being Difficult

Like it or not, clients are the ones fuelling your business with cash—the cash you need to keep your business operations alive, pay your employees (good or bad), and, well, *make profit*.

Therefore, simply telling a difficult client that they are

hard to deal with is not an option.

Types of Difficult Clients

Knowing the types of difficult clients can help you deal with situations better, just like in the case of difficult employees, so let's take a closer look at some of the main typologies.

1. The Know-Nothing. This client really doesn't know anything about what they want, how they want it and, many times, *when* they want it. It is important to be patient with this client, explain the options, and then give your agreement in writing to them, so that no detail is left out.

2. The Squeezer. This person wants to squeeze just a little bit more into a project every time they contact you. And the main issue with this is that they frequently expect it to be included in the initial quote you gave them. It is crucial to be firm with this typology of client and only add extras to your project if they agree to pay upfront.

3. The Rusher. This client will invariably send you super-mega-ultra urgent requests. They don't need it done by tomorrow, they need it three days ago. And they always follow the same pattern. If their expectations are unrealistic, make sure you relay this to them in a way that is polite and firm.

4. The Mind Changer. This client will have no deadline at first, and once the project starts, they will suddenly remember that it has to be done tomorrow. To avoid this kind of situation (especially with clients who show a pattern in this direction), agree on a timeline and have it delivered to them in writing. This way, they cannot challenge the agreement they made with you.

5. The Laissez-Faire-er. This person will leave you *full* creative freedom. And by *full*, please understand that they will not give you any kind of instructions, *at all*. This can be obviously problematic, as you will not know how to proceed in a variety of situations. DO make sure to ask them for details and make the instructions clear before you proceed with your work on this project. It will help you avoid endlessly negative emails in the future.

6. The Naysayer. Most often, this person will not tell you what they actually want (because not even they know it). At the same time, though, they will eagerly and quickly point out that they don't want what you have already done. Again, making the instructions crystal clear with the client (and having them in written form) is extremely important when dealing with this kind of people.

7. The Penny Hoarder. This client is the keeper of the treasury. He/she will look at every single penny added on a quote and ask if anything will cost them extra. When dealing with this kind of client, it is important to not *leave it be*; if they cannot pay for the extras, you simply cannot do it.

8. The Micro-Manager. This is the kind of person who will come with instructions so specific that you will actually wonder what your role is in all of this. He/she cares so much about the project that he/she will constantly micro-manage it to the point of driving you crazy. When it comes to these clients, the best way is to be frank when they are asking for something that simply cannot be done.

9. The Never-Sleeper. You have serious doubts this person ever sleeps. They send emails at 4 am, they schedule their meetings long after hours, and they even want to have chats with you on the phone on Christmas Day. It is essential that you establish boundaries with these people and let them know that you work on a schedule. During that time frame, you are all there to help them, but anything beyond that time frame will not allow you to actually reply to emails and answer the phone.

10. The Know-Better. This man (or woman) is an expert at everything. They are accountants by profession, and marketers, architects, programmers and nurses by... internet. They think they know better and that they could do it better and quicker, but for some reason, they always call for your help. When their suggestions are unrealistic, be honest and tell them that it simply cannot be done as they think it can be done.

11. The Multi-Headed Decision Maker. This client is like Cerberus, but instead of guarding the Gates of Hell, they guard the gates of "which-comma-goes-where-in-this-text." More often than not, they make decisions *as a group*, because their internal procedures do not allow them to do otherwise. It is vital to be patient with this Cerberus of the client world and to make sure that you only communicate with *one* of the members of the committee. Otherwise, chaos can very quickly ensue.

12. The Whack-A-Mole. This client disappears for months at a time. But when they come back, you know it, because they have a thousand and one requests, all due by the end of the day. To make sure you don't break under their negative behaviour, apply the same rules for them as you do for everyone: if anything takes a few days to

be processed for each and every client, it should take nothing less for this client.

Of course, these are some of the most *common* typologies of clients. Sometimes, their personalities are combined, and you might have to deal with someone who disappears like a mole for months only to pop up suddenly and come to you with nit-picky requests that simply drive you and your team crazy.

Patience is key when dealing with such clients. They are the way they are because someone encouraged this behaviour in them. Someone like you perhaps allowed them to be like this and didn't tell them things cannot be done as fast as they want them or based on terms as ambiguous as they have.

How to Actually Deal with Bad Clients

Although the situation might frequently feel inescapable, it is important to acknowledge the fact that dealing with bad clients without completely losing them *is* actually possible.

There are a lot of things you can do about difficult clients, and in the following I have gathered some of the most important tips to keep in mind when you have to deal with any of the aforementioned typologies (or any other type of bad client, for that matter):

1. Don't be afraid. The moment you are afraid is the moment you lose. Fear can be a very powerful motivator in making people do things, but it can also be a wall between you and properly communicating with bad clients.

2. Listen actively. If your client is angry, it is important to tone down the situation as much as you can. Reflective listening can help because it will give the other party the feeling they are properly understood. Constantly reinforcing the discussion with phrases like "I understand" and "I see" can really help bridge the communication gap and mend the problem.

3. Clients have biases too. Sometimes, they might have had a very bad experience with a vendor just like you. So they will be sceptical when it comes to your services, as well. When you feel a client is being apprehensive, try to ask questions to get down to the root of the problem.

4. Walk a mile in their shoes. When a customer does not understand the features of your services or products, try to look at the matter from the point of view of a beginner. It will make it easier for you to explain everything in a way that is easy to understand for the client.

5. Split the problem. When the issue the client is bringing forward is very difficult, it is of the

utmost importance to make sure you chunk it down to smaller, more manageable bites, and then deal with them one by one. The same tactic is employed in project management styles like Scrum or Kanban, for example: everything is sliced down to very small tasks that can be easily handled and delivered.

6. Acknowledge the fact that anger is, well, natural. It so happens that it is a mechanism wired into our brains and that its evolution with us is tightly connected to how we used to bargain. When a customer is angry, you might feel tempted to justify yourself. However, that is the worst thing you can do. Instead, you should stay calm and assess the situation with as much coolness as you can. Just as with everything anger-related, your customer feels that way because they think they have been undervalued. Listen to them, acknowledge their pain, and promise to come back with a solution. There is just no other way to deal with this.

7. Be careful how you choose your words! Really, even a bad couple of words can completely shift the dynamics of your communication. So, do take your time to think things through and formulate answers that will not escalate the situation even more.

8. Be humble, but clear. Adding a short "from my limited experience" at the beginning of a paragraph that will push back against what the client has requested can soften the blow and make you seem more approachable. Thus, it will help you prevent nasty situations.

9. Always be specific. When possible, use any kind of quantifiable measurement to help your client understand why something may not be possible, or why something has to be done a certain way.

10. Keep in mind that acknowledgement and agreement are not one and the same thing. Just because you acknowledge the fact that a client is in a rush, it doesn't mean you can actually deliver their product or service twice as fast.

11. Accept that sometimes, you simply cannot do anything. That is that. Some people are just too hard to deal with, and if you reach that conclusion, it is quite important to consider whether or not it is actually worth it to continue working with that client. Yes, you can fire clients. You should do everything you can to avoid it, just as you would with employees, but when the situation gets out of control and one bad client makes a bad day, a bad week, a bad month, and a bad trimester, drawing all your energy towards them, it might be time to let them go.

Without doubt, every situation is different in its own way, so it is of the utmost importance that you handle them gracefully and tactfully. Don't give in to unreasonable client requests—accepting them once means you will accept them for the entire duration of your collaboration. Be firm, polite, and specific about the reasons that make something unfeasible. Most bad clients will come to reason!

When Your Partner Is Being Difficult

While dealing with difficult clients can be hard, so is dealing with a difficult partner. You are more or less on the same level with them because you have actually *partnered* with them in this whole endeavour.

At the same time, it is more than worth mentioning that not dealing with this situation tactfully can lead to tension between you and your partner, and consequently, it can lead to even more difficult situations, including the dissolution of the partnership.

Some of the tips you want to keep in mind when handling a difficult partner include the following:

1. Plan ahead. The more you plan ahead your meetings, discussions, KPIs, and projects, the more you will avoid contradictory chats with

your partner. So, try to plan everything way before it happens!

2. Don't judge. This stands just as valid when you are dealing with a difficult partner as it does when you are dealing with a difficult employee. Start with the presumption that the person in front of you is not guilty. This will help you maintain your positivity and it will help you create a communication bridge between you and the difficult person in front of you.

3. Don't be afraid to address the issue. Just as with a difficult employee, allowing matters to fly by as they are will only make things worse; it could potentially have an effect on the team, on how you connect to your partner, and on how you can resolve the situation. The more time it takes for you to act, the more the problem will grow into something that is less manageable.

4. When you discuss matters with your partner, be sure you are fully dedicated to listening. This is extremely important because it will impact how your partner perceives the entire discussion. If you listen, you will avoid disputes and you will avoid anything that might trigger your partner to think you are looking for a fight. Listening well means that you are not busy formulating your response while the other person is talking. You

need to have the confidence and self-assurance to simply listen, with a goal of understanding and communicating respect, trusting that you will have the right things to say when it's your turn to speak.

5. Don't allow yourself to be bummed by the situation. Given that you started this whole partnership in full hope that your business will prosper, it is completely understandable why you might feel that your partner's behaviour will actually ruin everything you have been trying to build. However, you shouldn't allow the situation to put you down. Most of the time, behaviours can be corrected, but in order for that to happen, you will first and foremost have to take action (which circles us back to point #3 here).

6. You don't *have to be* right. In fact, this is quite harmful and it can turn into a negative behaviour on its own. Oftentimes, there is a variety of solutions to a problem or a question. Each of us usually only sees one dimension of a problem. But when we work together and combine our perspectives and ideas, we often arrive at a better solution. Address the issue with your partner bearing an open heart and an open mind; don't turn this into a situation that could potentially escalate. Instead, by surrendering the goal of being right, you may create the opportunity for a

breakthrough in a problem area and thereby create new energy and unity for your partnership.

7. Focus on the positives. There are some very specific things that brought you and your partner together. It may be the fact that he/she is a good programmer and you are a good manager. If may simply be the fact that you used to be very good friends and you always dreamed of building a business together. Whatever it is, focus on that when you discuss matters with your partner to find a solution.

8. Don't play the blame game. Even if it actually *is* your partner's fault that things went downhill, you shouldn't put this on them. Truthfully, there are always two parts involved in any kind of fight or divorce, so you should acknowledge that you too might have some sort of part to play in the situation. Sure, you have never pushed your partner into developing bad behaviour, but even so, there might have been things you inadvertently did or said that made it more likely for them to develop this behaviour. The whole point is that blaming the other party will only lead to conflict, and at this point, that is the last thing you want.

9. Try to get to the bottom of the issue. When partners start behaving negatively, there is

frequently much more to it. They may have lost interest in the business. They may find that they are doing too much of the work and think you are doing nothing at all. They might be dissatisfied with your management methods. Whatever it is, getting down to the root cause of their behaviour will allow you to actually find a solution together.

10. Don't be afraid to bring help if you need it. Sometimes, situations get so dire that communication is simply ineffective. If it comes to this, do consider the fact that you may have to bring in an external party to mediate the communication between you and your partner and help you find a solution that is viable to both parties.

Seeing a partner develop negative behaviour can be really disappointing, from a number of points of view. The fact that you had such grand hopes of your relationship with them, the fact that someone can transform so rapidly into a person you simply don't like—there are, indeed, a lot of reasons to be really disappointed in the whole situation.

However, it is important that you refuse to give up. Like romantic relationships, business partnerships take effort to survive the sands of time, so don't allow one big fight to put both of you off. Communicate and find a solution together! In my experience, this is more than feasible in the majority of situations!

When Your Boss Is Being Difficult

Dealing with a bad client is one thing. Dealing with a partner you have fallen off with is a different thing.

But when you have to deal with a boss torn out of a nightmare scenario, you know it's going to be more than just difficult.

On the one hand, you cannot come to work every day and constantly handle your boss's negative behaviour. On the other hand, you cannot lose your job over an honest discussion with your boss either.

Believe it or not, there are tactics you can use when you have to deal with a difficult boss. Here are some of the most important ones:

1. Assess your situation. I am not trying to put the blame on you, but before you jump into taking action against your boss's difficult behaviour, it is important that you assess your situation. Are you actually dealing with a really bad boss? They are out there, just like bad employees, bad clients, and bad partners. But before you judge someone, try to understand if there might be an underlying

reason your boss is acting the way he/she does.

For instance, they might deal with a bad boss themselves. They might have orders from "upstairs" that push them over the edge. They might have trouble at home. Or they might simply have trouble adjusting to a new leadership position.

Try to look objectively at your boss for a few days and take mental notes of how many times they misbehave and how many times they are doing things right. This will give you a good indication of whether or not you are actually dealing with a difficult boss.

2. Try to not let it get to you. Regardless of what your boss's motivation may be for behaving poorly, don't let their actions and words affect your work. This will only give them further reason to pick on you and even to start placing the blame of a poorly performing team on you. You need to keep a professional stance at all times!

3. If you have already noticed a pattern in your boss's bad behaviour, try to stay a step ahead of them at all times. For instance, if you know they will micro-manage you on every task, prepare reports before they even come to you to see how things are going.

4. Keep thinking positively. I know I have

emphasised this a lot in the book, but it is one of the parts I have learned to be essential for the success of the Zero Tolerance approach—regardless of who it is applied on.

For instance, if you assume your manager knows everything just because they are a manager, then you are in for a disappointment. Instead, stay positive and acknowledge that nobody knows it all—not even your boss. This means that you will set your expectations correctly and that you will not be disappointed by your boss's actions as much.

5. Be the informal leader of the team. One of the worst parts about dealing with a bad boss is that they are frequently incompetent—not just in terms of management, but also in the industry you work.

Of course, it is not absolutely mandatory that a project manager in an IT company is also a great programmer, but when bad management is combined with bad knowledge of the industry's specificities, disaster can ensue.

If you know you are very good at what you do, you can always act as the informal leader of your team. This *does not* mean you have to boss people around and become a negative employee yourself. Instead, it means that you should help those around you whenever they need guidance. It means that you should step up when requirements "from above" are unrealistic. And it means you should constantly provide support for the other team members to grow.

6. Is anger management your boss's biggest issue? Most of the time, people with anger management problems are triggered by very specific things. If you have spotted those triggers, do everything you can to avoid them. It will simply make your life easier and create less negativity in the workplace.

7. Don't badmouth your boss. It is far too risky for a long list of reasons. Telling your workmates about the problems you have with your boss could reach your boss's ears, for example. And even if it doesn't, it will create even more negative behaviour in your workplace, which is obviously not what you are aiming for.

8. The ball is in your court. No matter how you look at this, you are the only one who can actually manage your relationship with your boss. Your teammates, your loved one, even your best friend at work and even the boss himself/herself—nobody else can do it for you. So, instead of allowing negative behaviour to turn you sour and bitter on a daily basis, step up and accept that the ball is in your hands. YOU have the power to change this, one way or another.

9. It's really negative to think of this, but sometimes, the only two solutions you have is to either fire your boss (or, better said, have them fired) or leave that job. If the latter option is just not feasible for you (and you are entitled to feel this way), then you should start a process where you clearly show your boss's boss just how bad their behaviour is. You could bring them into a situation where your boss will display his/her worst behaviour. Or you could take the same path as the one we have described regarding bad employees: documenting every situation and taking it upstairs.

It is crucial that you are very secretive and tactful about this. A wrong move could send your career spiraling down. So be extremely careful with the whole situation.

10. Don't disconnect and disengage from your boss. You need to put in all the effort you can to make sure you don't burn the communication channel between you and your boss. The moment that happens, you might turn into a bad employee in their eyes, and you may soon be perceived as the issue, instead of the victim.

11. Try to get yourself transferred to another team. If you simply cannot cope with your boss, but don't necessarily want to change your job, try to see if you can get transferred to another team. If

the issue is related to your supervisor per se (and not company culture, for example), it is likely that you will find a more peaceful environment on another team.

12. Change your job and make sure to avoid future horrible bosses. The great part about an open market is that you can always change your job. Of course, when the time comes to sit for an interview, you should provide a different reasoning for *why* you are changing your job. You don't want to badmouth your current workplace and its management.

Changing jobs might seem radical, but it can actually be the best option when you have been dragging yourself to work every day, feeling absolutely miserable about every second you spend there. Unfortunately, this can happen, and it can ruin your passion for what you do. It can make you inefficient, and in turn, it can make you become a negative employee yourself.

So, it's probably best if you jump ships while you still have the time. DO make sure to spot any kind of potentially negative behaviour in the people you interview with. You really don't want to go from one bad boss to another!

Dealing with difficult bosses can be a true challenge for just about anyone. Even the most positive person in the world can feel attacked by a boss who just doesn't cope with them, by a boss who is incompetent, or by a boss who simply has a very bad anger management issue. That is precisely why it's so important for you to take action!

Thinking Time

Everyone has to deal with difficult people at least once in their life, but have you ever had to deal with a bad client?

What was your approach? Were you proactive?

Even more, what are some of the most common bad client profiles you have encountered? How about bad partners or bad bosses?

Think of how you reacted back then and how you would react knowing everything you know now, after reading this book.

Summary

It's one thing to work with a leader who constantly pushes you further by providing you constructive feedback. And it's different when you work with a boss who has his/her bad moments.

But when your boss is constantly diminishing you, micro-managing you without reason, and making your work life a living hell with all kinds of unreasonable requests, you need to take action. At first, you will want to fix whatever is left of your relationship with your boss. If that doesn't work, you might try to either move to another team or, in the worst case scenario, take your boss's negativity upstairs, to their own manager.

And if everything fails, you should leave the company. You spend one-third of your life at work. You don't have to spend it in misery, feeling like you are constantly pushed to the wall with no real reason.

Regardless of whether you have had to deal with a really awful employee, a very demanding and mean client, a partner who has started turning on you, or a boss who has serious anger management problems, you know just how difficult it can be to move past fear, comfort and convenience, or simply past the thought of failing in your endeavours.

It can take weeks or even months before you gather up the courage to take action against a person who has been poisoning your days with negative behaviours.

But when it happens, you need to follow through with it. The Zero Tolerance approach is there to provide you with balanced support in these situations. Far from being a theory that will turn you into a dictator (as a boss) or a Rebel (as an employee), Zero Tolerance is about stopping the flow of negativity into your life.

Yes, getting past the anxiety and discomfort of that first discussion you have with an employee or that first direct email you send a client can be downright scary. Take this from someone who's been there on all fences—as a manager, as an employee, as a bad client's main point of contact.

It's not easy. But it has to be done if you don't want to spend the rest of your work life in misery, remorse, and frustration!

Conclusion

Unfortunately, there is just no way to avoid difficult people altogether because, well, people are people.

In many ways, you should be actually thankful for the existence of negative people. Just like in life, the sun shines brighter after a rainy day, so negative behaviours will only help you realise the power of the positive people in your life and just how great your work is because of them.

Even more, sometimes the worst employees can turn into the biggest rock stars when they are managed properly. Someone who is late and admonished for it, then praised for having changed their behaviour has good chances of becoming a genuinely loyal employee. Someone who used to complain a lot might actually become a much more positive person if he/she is shown just how much better it feels to be positive about your work and the people surrounding you for eight straight hours every day.

Because, yes, we spend one third of our lifetime at work. Both you and the people you work with deserve to have a great time! I won't lie, it is true that most of us would much rather spend our time otherwise, but when you like what you do and when you are surrounded by positive people at work, life just gets a little better. Not to mention, the business prospers and becomes a flourishing one that feeds more people (and better, at that!).

Zero Tolerance is not about turning yourself into a dictator. Rather than that, it is about turning yourself into a mentor—for those who are great workers and for the bad sheep, as well. It is extremely important to stay positive about your Zero Tolerance approach because negativity can affect you directly as well.

Don't think of the fact that you have to let someone go. Think of the fact that it will stop affecting everyone else on your team and how much better they will feel as a result, even when it might come as a shock to them that you have actually fired someone.

Don't think of the fact that you could have given them another chance. Think of the fact that you gave them a second chance the first time around.

Don't think of the fact that negativity has affected your workplace. Be glad that you have managed to fix the situation and turn it around before it was too late!

The Zero Tolerance approach is, in my humble opinion, the *only* approach. Closing an eye once or twice might be OK, but doing it repeatedly means you are disrespecting yourself and all the other people who are working hard, every day, every year, to grow the business and make it better for everyone else.

Think of it this way: you wouldn't reinforce bad behaviour in a child, right? If they constantly jump in puddles of mud when they are wearing their sneakers, you wouldn't encourage them to continue doing it, right? And you wouldn't allow this to fly too many times either, right? In the end, the health of that child would be at stake—and their future too, given that bad behaviours are frequently born in childhood.

The same goes for bad behaviours in the workplace. As a manager, you sometimes have to be a parent for your team, and one that doesn't reinforce bad behaviours.

I am totally one for kindness and care. I genuinely believe the best managers are those who truly care about their teams and guide their every step to see each and every member grow and shine.

At the same time, though, *caring* is not about ignoring the bad apples, just like it isn't about it when it comes to parenting. It is about seeing the larger picture, about being fair, and about being true to yourself and what you stand for, as well as what the entire company culture stands for.

Address the types of problems presented in this book as early as you can, address them fairly, try to control your subjectivity and biases (be they negative or positive), and create action plans that are personalised to each individual. Hopefully, you don't have 99 problems in a team of 100, so you should dedicate the time to actually finding a customised solution for each of them. Because, to circle back to what I was saying earlier, everyone is different, so it makes all the sense in the world that you address everyone differently too.

To end on a high (and positive!) note, I will trace back to an old adage that originated in the British military: Proper Prior Planning Prevents Piss-Poor Performance.

It just is what it is. And your job, as a manager, is to do exactly that: plan. This applies not only to planning the KPIs and the deliverables, but also to planning how you treat people, how you reward them, and, at times, how you admonish them, too.

I genuinely wish this book to be of great use for you in the future. Believe it or not, there *are* teams that function seamlessly and are filled with positive energies every day. I have seen it with my own eyes—and oh, my, how can it change *everything*!

Good luck in your endeavours! Stay patient, stay kind, stay strong and stop allowing negative people to hijack all the amazing things you and your team are building!

You deserve this! Your team deserves this!

References

Benson, B. (2016.) You are almost definitely not living in reality because your brain doesn't want you to. *Quartz*. Retrieved from https://qz.com/776168/a-comprehensive-guide-to-cognitive-biases/.

McCarthy, D. Tips on how to deal with difficult employees. (2018). *The Balance Careers*. Retrieved from https://www.thebalancecareers.com/how-to-deal-with-difficult-employees-2276071.

Mcleod, S. (2017). The Milgram shock experiment. *Simply Psychology*. Retrieved from https://www.simplypsychology.org/milgram.html

Mcleod, S. (2018). Solomon Asch—conformity experiment. *Simply Psychology*. Retrieved from https://www.simplypsychology.org/asch-conformity.html

Pogosyan, M. Can emotions be controlled?. (2018). *Psychology Today*. Retrieved from https://www.psychologytoday.com/intl/blog/between-cultures/201811/can-emotions-be-controlled.

Printed in Poland
by Amazon Fulfillment
Poland Sp. z o.o., Wrocław